WHAT PEOPLE

PAGAN PORTA

C000313056

This is a very readable, user-friendly book giving a taster of a broad range of meditation practices. Pragmatic, highly usable, and with plenty of inspiration and jumping off points, this is a great place to start if you want to explore meditation as a Pagan.
Nimue Brown, author of *Druidry and Meditation*

Rachel Patterson has written an exuberant and free-spirited introduction to a subject often treated with undue deference and solemnity. She gives her readers permission to sample the smorgasbord of the world's traditions, providing a stimulus to craft their own practice and/or connect with relevant communities and teachers.
James Nichol, author of *Contemplative Druidry*

Pagan Portals
Meditation

Pagan Portals
Meditation

Rachel Patterson

Winchester, UK
Washington, USA

First published by Moon Books, 2015
Moon Books is an imprint of John Hunt Publishing Ltd., Laurel House, Station Approach,
Alresford, Hants, SO24 9JH, UK
office1@jhpbooks.net
www.johnhuntpublishing.com
www.moon-books.net

For distributor details and how to order please visit the 'Ordering' section on our website.

Text copyright: Rachel Patterson 2014

ISBN: 978 1 78535 030 6
Library of Congress Control Number: 2015943097

A CIP catalogue record for this book is available from the British Library.

Design: Lee Nash

Printed and bound by CPI Group (UK) Ltd, Croydon, CR0 4YY, UK

We operate a distinctive and ethical publishing philosophy in all
areas of our business, from our global network of authors to
production and worldwide distribution.

CONTENTS

Who am I?

I am a witch...have been for a very long time. Not the green skinned warty kind obviously...the real sort, but I am also a working wife and mother who has also been lucky enough to write and have published a book or three. I love to learn, I love to study and I have done so from books, online resources, schools and wonderful mentors over the years and I still continue to learn each and every day, but I have learnt the most from actually getting outside and doing it.

I like to laugh...and eat cake...

I am High Priestess of the Kitchen Witch Coven and an Elder at the online Kitchen Witch School of Natural Witchcraft.

My craft is a combination of old religion witchcraft, Wicca, Kitchen Witchery, green witchery and folk magic. My heart is that of a Kitchen Witch. I am blessed with a wonderful husband, lovely children, a fabulous family and good friends.

Websites and Social Media

My website: www.rachelpatterson.co.uk

Facebook: www.facebook.com/rachelpattersonbooks

My personal blog: www.tansyfiredragon.blogspot.co.uk

Email: tansyfiredragon@yahoo.com

www.kitchenwitchhearth.net

www.kitchenwitchuk.blogspot.co.uk

www.facebook.com/kitchenwitchuk

www.thekitchenwitchcauldron.blogspot.co.uk

What is Meditation?

Meditation is an amazing way to relax, to de-stress, to get answers from your subconscious and to connect with deity, spirits and totem animals. But rest assured, you don't need to be able to bend like a pretzel, burn incense or be able to 'om'...although you can if you want to.

This book is an introductory one that will hopefully open up the varied and diverse world of meditation for you and prompt you to seek out more information...

There are many ways and lots of different forms of meditation; the key is in finding the right one for you.

I try to meditate every day, even if it is just for a few minutes. It relaxes me, de-stresses and brings me back focused and centred. And I do know how hard it can be sometimes to find even five minutes of time to yourself, especially if you are a working mum (or dad) with children...life can be hectic, but even if you can manage to steal a couple of minutes to yourself by hiding in the toilet (don't forget to lock the door) just to close your eyes and focus it will be worth it.

I would like to mention here that meditation, while brilliant for most people, won't suit absolutely everyone and it may be that some forms of meditation work better for you than others. If you suffer from any kind of mental illness or acute depression it might be worth seeking out a meditation group with an experienced teacher first to give you advice and guide you.

There are many types of meditation and a lot of them are very similar across different cultures, but with different names. Some of them sound very fancy and the odd one or two may require religious dedication, but please rest assured that you don't have to sign up to a cult or become a monk to be able to successfully meditate. I have listed some forms here, but this is by no means complete. Have a read through and see if any particular practice catches your eye, but don't worry if it doesn't because at the end of the day all you need is a quiet spot where you can sit or stand comfortably and allow your mind to do the rest. The list is not in any particular order other than alphabetic because I am a slight control freak...

Ascension meditation – Perhaps the ultimate goal of meditation? This is to achieve pure enlightenment and self realisation through meditative practice, to reach the stage of ascending to a union with the Divine.

Apophatic meditation – Meditation without images or visualisations, concentrating instead on divine love that fills the world. In this state you are reflective, but not stressed, enabling you to ground and find balance.

Breathing meditation – This is where you focus on your breath, concentrating on each breath you take in and each breath you exhale and connecting with your life force.

Cleansing meditation – Useful to cleanse your chakras or your aura.

Contemplative inquiry meditation – You have a question, ask it and then reflect upon it, allowing your subconscious to throw answers or perhaps even more questions in...

Day-dreaming – Don't discount this because it is in a way a form of meditation.

Gratitude meditation – A practice that focuses on contentment, happiness and joy through feeling total gratitude and being grateful for all that you have in life.

Guided meditation – Following a script that you have read before starting or listening to a recorded meditation that takes you on a specific journey.

Heart meditation – Focusing your practice on opening your heart and sacral chakra to increase your ability to love and to release.

Hedge riding – Similar to shamanic journeying where a hedge witch journeys to the Otherworld/Underworld realms.

Intentionality meditation – This involves a prayer or blessing. You say your prayer and then just listen quietly.

Kasina meditation – A Buddhist practice of concentration meditation to settle the mind, which involves visualising multiple objects associated with the four elements and four colours with the addition of enclosed space and bright light initially, with a further 30 objects. Discs are used to focus on for each one until the practitioner has an image in their mind.

Kinhin – A walking meditation practiced in between long periods of sitting meditation. The practitioner walks clockwise around the room holding their hands with one hand closed in a fist and the other grasping to cover the fist. During the meditation each step is taken after each full breath. The pace of the walk can vary from very slow with several steps to each breath or much faster.

Mantra meditation – Repeating a word or a phrase in your mind or softly out loud over and over, this takes you into a kind of trance. A mantra is not an affirmation, but a syllable or word used to focus your mind. Mantras are used in Hindu, Buddhist, Jainism, Sikhism and Taoism traditions. Mantra meditation is often called om meditation.

Metta meditation or loving kindness meditation – Metta is a Pali word that translates as kindness, benevolence and good will. This is another practice from Buddhism, especially Theravada and Tibetan. Practicing this form of meditation offers the benefits of boosting your empathy, developing positive emotions through compassion and becoming more self accepting. For this meditation you focus on your mind and heart and generate feelings of kindness and benevolence. You start by developing these feelings and emotions for yourself and then move on to others. You wish well-being to all and send love and good will to each and every person on the planet and then the planet itself.

Mindfulness meditation – This meditation requires you to just sit quietly and intentionally observe your thoughts, emotions and feelings, not judging, but just watching and focusing on the present moment. This form of meditation is adapted from traditional Buddhist practices, especially Vipassana, but also takes influence from Vietnamese Zen Buddhism. Mindfulness is the common translation for the Buddhist term 'sati Anapanasati', which means 'mindfulness of breathing'. You can practice this mindfulness during your everyday activities, a kind of daily living meditation that requires you to pay attention to what is going on at any particular moment and being aware of what is happening, what you are saying, how you say your words, listening and paying attention.

Pathworking/journeying – Specific meditations to seek answers or healing.

Planetary meditation – When several people from all across the world meditate at a set time of day, every day, to focus on world peace.

Pranayama – The regulation of your breathing. Used to calm the mind and prepare it for meditation. It is not exactly a meditation form on its own, but worth mentioning as the term is used a lot in meditation practices.

Qiqong (chi kung) – Qigong is a Chinese word that means 'life energy cultivation' and works with exercises for your mind and your body to bring health, meditation and martial arts training together. It includes slow body movements, inner focus and regulated breathing.

Seeking meditation – This can be used when you seek to consult with a deity or a spirit animal.

Self enquiry – Atma vichara, which is the Sanskrit term meaning 'self enquiry' or to investigate our true nature; the age-old 'Who am I?' question. This practice aims to discover your true self and true being. You will need to ask 'Who am I?' within yourself and reject the initial verbal answers, the question is used to fix your attention, but you must become one with it and go deep...

Shamanic journeying – Performed by shamanic practitioners who enter a trance-like state quite often through hypnotic drumming and/or dancing to enter the realms of spirit/ Otherworld to seek wisdom and healing.

Spiritual meditation – Bit of a giveaway in the title...meditating on your spirit.

Tantra – I know what you are thinking...but most tantra practices have nothing to do with hours of sex (sorry, I know you are disappointed now...) The text Vijnanabhairava Tantra lists 108 different meditations, a lot of them are for the advanced practitioner as they require absolute focus of mind, but they cover a lot of familiar ground such as focusing on objects, the space between two thoughts, the inside of your head, the sound of your heart and the universe.

Taoist meditation – Daoism is a Chinese philosophy and religion that dates back to Lao Tzu in the 6th century BC. It focuses on living in harmony with nature. The meditation generates transformation and circulation of inner energy to quieten and unify the body, mind and spirit ultimately to find inner peace. It can also include improving your health. The practices include:

- **Emptiness meditation** – Sitting quietly and emptying all images and thoughts to experience inner quiet and emptiness.
- **Breathing meditation (Zhuanqi)** – Focusing on your breath to unite your mind and qi.

Neiguan (inner observation, inner vision) – Visualising the inside of your body and mind including the squishy bits, your inner deities and your qi (life force). It is a process of getting to know the nature of your body.

Tai chi meditation – Often referred to as 'movement meditation'. You move your chi or life force through your body to cleanse and clear out any negative energy through slow physical movements of your body.

Transcendental Meditation™ – This is a specific type of mantra meditation originating in the mid-1950s in India and introduced by Maharishi Mahesh Yogi. This form of meditation can only be learnt by paying one of the Transcendental Meditation licensed instructors (although if you promise not to tell anyone you can find a lot of the mantras and more information by searching the internet…but I didn't tell you that). It is generally known that this form of meditation uses a personal mantra and involves practicing twice a day.

Vipassana meditation – Vipassana is a Pali word meaning 'insight' or 'clear seeing'. This is a traditional Buddhist practice that originally dates back to the 6th century BC. Vipassana meditation that is popular now comes from the Teravada Buddhist tradition. Generally with this practice you start with mindfulness of breath and move on to clear insight on your bodily sensations and mental visions. This is an excellent form of meditation to help you ground and become connected to your body and inner being.

Visualisation – Focusing on just one image, it might be a candle, a crystal or an image from nature, allows your mind to concentrate on one thing and brings calm and stillness.

Yoga meditation – For me yoga is a combination of body movements, but if done in the right way can also be very meditative. Classic yoga can be divided into sections; conduct (yamas and niyamas), postures (asanas), breathing exercises (pranayama) and meditation (pratyahara, dharana, dhyana, samadhi). There are many different types of meditation practices that can be used during yoga including:

- **Third eye meditation** – Focusing on your third eye to help silence the mind and subconsciously looking at that spot.
- **Chakra meditation** – The practitioner focuses on each chakra in turn using visualisation and mantras specific to each individual chakra.
- **Gazing meditation (trataka)** – This involves focusing on an object such as a candle or an image.
- **Kundalini meditation** – Quite a complex practice the goal of which is to awaken your kundalini energy which lies at

the base of your spine. You should work with a qualified yogi for this practice.

- **Sound meditation (nada yoga)** – Focusing on sound, which often starts with the use of calming music, but the goal is to hear your internal sounds (not your rumbling belly) to align yourself with your inner body and mind.

Zen meditation – Zazen is a type of meditation unique to Zen Buddhism. The zazen, which literally translates as 'seated meditation', is at the heart of the practice. Zen is the Japanese word for meditation. The essence of zazen is to not think, to go beyond thinking. To avoid having intentional thoughts and images, letting them pass by allowing you to become tranquil and at peace.

States of Consciousness

When you go into meditation or do any energy work you might notice that your state of consciousness changes. Moving into a different consciousness is one of the keys to working with energy or meditation.

If you change your state of consciousness as a voluntary action then you won't lose yourself. You will be able to still concentrate, still work with energy and still have your intent in place.

This state of consciousness was called gnosis by the ancient Greeks; it means knowledge. It is in this state that you can get answers, solve problems, connect with deity and have a psychic connection.

When we go about our daily lives – working, eating, driving etc – our brain waves are in a beta state. Once we move into meditation or working magic, if we have done it properly our brain waves move into an alpha state. It is a state of mind where we are relaxed, but still aware of what is going on around us. Being in this alpha state (like you are when you are in a day-dream) allows you to connect directly with your psychic mind. The next stage is theta brain waves; this is the level you are at when you enter a deep trance, and the stage you enter when you are asleep. Then you have delta, which is the level your brain waves are at when you are in a very deep sleep, a very deep trance or indeed a coma.

Our Minds

How many minds do you have? There is the old saying, 'I am in two minds,' but in actual fact we have three, although to be honest some days I am not sure I even have one… Understanding how our three minds work helps us to work with energy, magic, meditate and gain clarity.

Your Conscious Mind, Your Middle Self

The first mind I want to talk about is our conscious mind, the one we are probably most familiar with. This is where you will find your personality and your ego. This is the mind that deals with everyday life when we are awake.

The conscious mind houses our reason, our logic, and our ability to analyse and stay alert. It deals with life as a series of events in a timeline, one after another. It sees life as sorted into compartments – past, present and future. The conscious mind is actually pretty good at remembering past events, dealing with the present and working out what it wants for the future, all at the same time. You could say it is your 'multi-tasking mind'.

It is your conscious mind that works out what you want for yourself. It is limited though in that it does see things as linear, which doesn't allow us to work through large amounts of energy or information.

The Psychic Mind, Your Lower Self, Your Younger Self

The second mind I want to talk about is the psychic mind. This is where you will find the key to your magical and visualization abilities. It has no limitations. It works with intuition. Intuition leads us into our psychic abilities. Have you ever known who was at the door before you opened it, or known who was on the telephone before answering it? That is your psychic mind at work (unless you have caller identity or a door peep hole...that's cheating).

This mind is called the lower self because it comes from our unconscious and our subconscious. As we relax our logical conscious mind we move into our subconscious, which allows us to see things with greater insight.

Much as it might be a nice idea to always live in your subconscious, we need the balance of the conscious mind and the psychic mind to be able to function properly.

The minds work together in harmony...hopefully...

The Divine Mind, the Higher Self, the Older Self

The psychic mind works as a connection between the conscious mind and the divine mind, which is the third mind or the higher self (are you confused yet?).

The divine mind is our spirit, it is what connects us to the whole. You can call this mind the Goddess, the God, the Divine Spirit. This level is a super conscious, a higher self, an older self. It can see things from a higher perspective spiritually and mentally. It is not bound by linear time or logic. It is aware of all things, on all levels, at all times. The divine mind knows what the conscious mind can handle so it drip feeds information so as not to overwhelm.

It is the divine mind that controls our dreams and intuition; it uses the psychic mind to relay this information. These symbols and messages are then deciphered by the unconscious and the subconscious.

The aim is to bring these three minds together so that they work as a team, so they are perfectly aligned. Once you have done this magic, energy work and meditation will be so much easier.

A good little exercise to do each day is to visualise your three minds, or selves, in harmony. This will have a positive effect on how you feel. Spend a couple of minutes each day, bring the lower self to the middle self, the middle self to the higher self and the higher self to the lower self so that they all harmonise together. When you get used to this exercise you will become aware of any harmony and any conflicts that your three selves have and you will know where the internal conflicts are.

There are various ways of visualizing the harmony exercise such as: three bubbles merging into one, three people holding hands, three Goddesses (the Maiden, Mother and Crone), imagining yourself as a tree with the roots, the trunk and the branches as your three selves, three different colour candles melding into one...you get the idea...

Hints and Tips for Meditation

Firstly, make sure you are comfortable and won't be disturbed. You can sit quietly or put on some peaceful music. Sometimes I just close my eyes, sometimes I sit in front of a lit candle and focus on the flame.

Either way you need to start with your breathing; take several long deep breaths in and out. As you breathe in, visualise you are breathing in a pure white cleansing light that fills your body; as you breathe out visualise all the stresses and worries leaving your body. Do this several times until you start to feel calm and at ease. An alternative is to visualise yourself walking down four or five steps. With each step you get deeper into the meditation, casting off worries as you take each step.

Then the choice is yours – you can either go to the sacred space in your mind if you already have one, or make a sacred space for yourself. Visualise somewhere that you feel happy and restful in – a field, a forest, on the beach, at the ocean – some place that you will feel totally at ease in. Over time you can visit this sacred space often and add to the area, you may even find new things appear all by themselves. It will be your own space, the place that is special to you, somewhere that you can visualise as your safe haven. This is the place I go to in my meditations last thing at night, this is the place where I sit to go over the events of the day with my animal spirit guides.

Or, you can use a guided meditation. Either read one over in your mind several times until you are familiar with it before you sit down to meditate and let your mind take you through it once in meditation or, as I do, use a mobile phone or iPod and sit with the earphones in and let the voice on the recording guide you through the meditation.

Drumming and music are also good ways to meditate, something with a regular steady beat, but not too 'busy'.

Once you come to the end of your meditation you need to make sure you bring yourself back to reality slowly, as coming out of meditation abruptly can cause headaches. Focus on your breathing again and slowly flex your fingers and your toes or use the step method, but in reverse, each step taken brings you closer to the real world again.

Meditation is a very useful tool to give you peace for a few moments each day, to release stress and worries and to give you clarity and focus. If you have a problem or an issue that needs some thought, try meditating on it.

These suggestions might seem obvious but just in case…these things help…

Avoid noisy distractions…so turn your phone off (unless you are using it to play meditation music through obviously). Turn off the TV!

Understand that meditation space does not necessarily mean silence, there may well be outside noises such as the dog next door barking, school children playing outside etc. Just acknowledge those are there and release them.

You need to be comfortable. Now, this doesn't mean you have to pop on your harem pants and Lycra yoga top, but you do need clothes that don't make you feel restricted. If you are at work taking a five-minute meditation break, just loosen your tie and slip your shoes off.

Know that you don't have to meditate for four hours straight…unless you are a Buddhist monk. Just five minutes is a good place to start, the more you practise the longer your meditations will become. Twenty minutes a day is perfect, but if you can only manage five minutes a day that is cool too. Don't keep checking your watch though, that will be totally distracting. If you are on a time schedule just set a gentle alarm on your phone or watch…not a blaring heavy metal sound that shocks you back into being, but some kind of tinkly 'Oooh, time to come back to reality' alarm.

I am not suggesting you do a complete yoga routine before you start, but just give your arms, neck and legs a bit of a stretch first as you will hopefully be sitting still for a bit. This just helps relax your muscles.

Sit or lie comfortably...you do not need to sit Buddha-style with your legs twisted because honestly that hurts even if you can get in that position in the first place. If you choose to sit on the floor, pop a cushion under your butt. But there is absolutely nothing wrong with sitting upright in a chair.

Meditation is traditionally performed with your eyes closed, but you don't have to. It does, however, help keep your mind focused and avoids distractions. If you choose to keep your eyes open allow them to unfocus and not particularly look at anything unless you choose to watch the flame of a candle or are looking at a crystal for instance.

Breathing is a key component of a successful meditation ...well of life really, but what I mean is specific meditation breathing, which we will look at further on.

Practising the art of visualisation can really help improve your meditation skills. You can do this by creating your own sacred space as I mentioned before, visualising a room/field/castle/open space and creating everything within that down to the smallest detail. You can also practise visualising an object in your mind, such as a piece of fruit – see it, examine every detail of the skin, leaves, stalk and colours then visualise taking a bite, how does it taste? You can do the same by visualising a flower and watching it grow from a bud into full bloom.

Try a walking meditation, which involves observing the movement of your feet and being aware of your connection to the earth. You will need a bit of space for this and outside is better than indoors. If you can remove your shoes as well that helps. Hold you head up and look straight ahead with your hands clasped in front of you. Take a slow step with your right foot, concentrating on the movement. After you take that first step, stop for a moment before taking the next step, only one foot should be moving at a time. Take seven steps forward in total then stop with your feet together. Pivot on your right foot and turn around. Continue walking again. Try to focus on the movement of your feet and nothing else.

I also find that releasing my inner child and grabbing the crayons can really help to focus and bring about a meditative state. Doodling works very well, but I love to draw and colour mandalas. Once you get into the repetitive rhythm of the colouring you will find that your brain switches into a state of peace and you can allow it to take you on a journey. You can purchase colouring books (even ones specifically for grownups) from book stores and the internet, but you can also download lots of free colouring pages and mandalas from the internet.

Mindfulness meditation can become part of your everyday life, when you get stressed during the day just stop for a few seconds and focus on your breathing to clear your mind from negative thoughts and emotions. Be mindful when you eat, focus on the food, what it tastes like, where it came from and the experience of eating it. Whatever you are doing throughout the day be aware of your thoughts; positive and negative and your body and how it feels.

Meditation is a journey, the purpose of which is to calm your mind, bring about inner peace and to eventually just 'be'. This journey may take you years...enjoy the ride. Don't worry at first about the quality of the meditation itself just focus on becoming happier, calmer and more at peace – if that is achieved then your meditation has worked.

Meditation Space/Altar

If you have room it is lovely to create a space to regularly use for your meditation. It may just be a favourite armchair with cushions and a blanket or you may be lucky enough to have space in a spare bedroom or conservatory to create a beautiful meditation room. Whatever you have available make sure it is warm, quiet and comfortable.

If you have the room for it, a meditation altar can really help to focus your mind. It could be a small side table, coffee table or even a little shelf. If you don't have space for something fixed you could use a small tea tray to bring out when you meditate (minus the teapot and cakes ...although...)

Place whatever items you feel drawn to on your altar. It might be a candle or two, some crystals, items from nature such as leaves, pebbles and shells, an image of deity or your totem animal and room for an incense burner. Go with what works for you, items will probably find their way there subconsciously anyway.

I have a meditation shawl, well actually it is more of a blanket. It is a beautiful soft material and has lots of fabulous colours in the pattern. I only use it when I meditate, either to sit on or to wrap around me. Somehow it helps as a bit of a prompt as if my brain sees it and says, 'There's the meditation shawl...time to focus.' And of course it keeps me warm because once you sit still for a while your body temperature usually drops a bit.

Get into Position

Do you have to twist your legs into a pretzel shape for the meditation to work? Um...no most definitely not because unless you are super bendy it would be incredibly uncomfortable and for a lot of us impossible anyway.

Here are some different positions used in Buddhist and Hindu traditions, some of them are simple, some may take practise and one or two of them I personally wouldn't attempt as I would get stuck and need assistance to be untangled...but go with what you find easiest and most comfortable:

Burmese position – This is where the legs are crossed with both knees resting flat on the floor with one ankle in front of the other (not over).

Half lotus position (Hankafuza) – You place your left foot onto the right thigh and tuck the right leg under your left thigh.

Full lotus position (Kekkafuza/Padmasana) – Place each foot onto the opposite thigh, this will probably be difficult at first and will most definitely be slightly painful on the first attempts, but with practise your leg muscles should loosen up. If it continues to be painful after a few days of practise don't do it! And definitely don't attempt this one if you have dodgy knees.

Easy pose (Sukhasana) – Sitting comfortably with crossed legged.

Accomplished pose (Siddhasana) – Sitting down, one heel is brought to the groin then the opposite ankle placed over the first leg with the toes and the heel of the second foot resting in the fold between the thigh and calf of the first leg beneath it while keeping the spine straight.

Kneeling position (Seiza) – Kneel with your hips resting on your ankles. This one can seem uncomfortable at first, but with practise it is quite a restful position.

Chair position – This doesn't really need any explanation does it? Just sit in a chair. It is perfectly acceptable to do so, just try to keep your back straight.

Standing position – If you can't sit comfortably for long periods of time then this one should suit you. Stand straight with your feet shoulder width apart, your heels slightly closer together than your big toes. Place your hands over your tummy, right hand over left and keep your knees loose (i.e. not locked straight).

Where you place your hands when meditating is also up to you, but there are a couple of traditional ways. One is to lay your hands on your knees palms facing up and open 'to receive'. Another way is to have your hands held in the 'cosmic mudra' (mudra is Sanskrit for seal or gesture) shape by placing your dominant hand palm upwards and holding your other hand (also palm up) with the thumbs just touching.

Zen meditation is often practiced using a special round cushion called a zafu; the cushion is used to raise the hips, forcing the knees to touch the ground. Having a cushion (it doesn't have to be round, one from your couch will suffice) can make sitting more comfortable, just tuck it under your butt.

Asana – in yoga 'asana' is literally 'the art of sitting still' and any posture that helps maintain and restore your well-being and help with your flexibility and health. Asanas are often referred to as 'yoga positions'. Any position that we sit or stand in is an asana whilst a yoga posture should really be called a 'yogasana'

Do it Your Way

At the end of the day I think the most important thing is to make sure you are comfortable and can stay in the chosen position for long enough to meditate.

If you find it easier to lie down on your bed, the sofa or the floor, then do it. If you prefer to just sit in your favourite armchair, chaise lounge or deck chair, then do that.

I often sit on a big cushion placed on the floor either with my legs loosely and, most importantly, comfortably crossed or I occasionally sit on the floor with my legs straight out in front of me.

Breathing Exercises

Adjusting your breathing when you meditate is essential as it will help you to enter a meditative 'state. There are several different breathing exercises that can be used, find one that suits you. And don't forget to really breathe in, big breathes that fill your belly. I think perhaps we have lost the art of breathing properly and no longer use our full lung capacity. Try it now...go on...place your hands on your tummy and then breathe in...does the breath really fill your lungs? Does your tummy move and your chest expand? Can you feel the movement through your hands of your belly moving as you breathe? Here are some breathing exercises that you might like to try that should help your meditative experience:

Three Relaxing Breaths
Sit with your mouth closed and your tongue gently resting on your upper palate.

Take a slow, deep breath in through your nose, breathe right down into your abdomen, feel it expand and your lungs fill completely.

As you breathe in, visualise your mind becoming clear and alert.

Hold that breath for a moment.

Then exhale slowly through your nose. As you exhale visualise stress flowing out of your body.

Hold your lungs empty for a moment.

Then repeat again twice.

Breath Awareness
Start this by just 'being'. Notice whatever is around you, take in the sounds, the scents, the thoughts and feelings, but don't do anything with them, just settle and 'be'. When you are ready

bring your attention to your breathing. Don't manipulate it, just be aware of it, notice as you breath in and breath out. Feel the air and how it makes your body feel. If you feel your mind wander just bring it back to your breathing. Let everything just come and go.

Breath Stillness

Using the breath awareness method above, once you are settled into the exercise start to notice the point where your breath stops being an inhale and becomes an exhale, that point of total stillness in between. Keep your attention focused on that tiny gap. Don't actually stop breathing obviously, just be aware of that moment in between.

Bellows Breath

Inhale and exhale rapidly through your nose, keeping your mouth closed (but relaxed). Your breaths in and out should be equal in duration, but as short as possible, this is a noisy exercise!

Aim for three in and out breath cycles per second if you can, it may take practise.

Breathe normally after each cycle.

Only do this for 10-15 seconds on your first try. Each time you try it see if you can last longer, up to a minute in total. This breathing exercise can make you quite light headed so make sure you are sitting down.

Relaxing

Place the tip of your tongue against the ridge just behind your upper front teeth and keep it there for this entire exercise. Exhale completely through your mouth making a whooshing sound.

Close your mouth and inhale quietly through your nose to a count of four (silently in your head).

Hold your breath for a count of seven.

Exhale completely through your mouth making a whooshing sound for a count of eight.

Now inhale again and repeat the cycle three more times.

Breath Counting

Take a few deep breaths to start, just naturally don't force it. Count inside your head 'one' as you exhale, the next time you exhale count to yourself 'two'…keep going until you reach five then start from one again. By only counting to five and starting the cycle again you bring focus, if you find you have started counting past five then your mind has wandered so just bring it back again.

Equal Breathing (Sama Vritti)

To start with, inhale for a count of four then exhale for a count of four, inhaling and exhaling through your nose (not your mouth). The more practised you get the longer you should be able to count for, aiming for six to eight counts per breath.

Alternate Nostril Breathing (Nadi Shodhana)

I know it sounds gross, doesn't it? But it works. This one is very calming and balancing and aims to unite the right and left sides of your brain. Hold your right thumb over your right nostril and inhale deeply through your left nostril. Once you have reached the peak of breathing in close off your left nostril with your ring finger then exhale through your right nostril. Continue the cycle inhaling through your right nostril, closing it off with your right thumb and exhaling through your left nostril. The instructions do sound complicated, but with practise it is easy to do and very effective. This one works best in the morning or during the day, done before bed time may make you feel energised and awake, which might not be advantageous.

Skull Shining Breath (Kapalabhati)

This one is probably best done after your meditation as it gives you a real boost of energy and has a total sugar rush effect ...without the sugar.

Start with a long, slow inhale followed by a quick powerful exhale that starts in your lower belly. Practise that for a few moments then quicken the pace to one inhale/exhale through your nose every couple of seconds for a total of ten breaths.

Progressive Relaxation

This works well to relax your whole body; close your eyes and focus on relaxing your muscles. Start with your toes and work up your body, mentally relaxing each muscle and joint – ankles, knees, thighs, hips, chest, arms, hands, neck etc – while taking deep, slow breaths. Breathe in through your nose and hold for a count of five while you tense your muscles, then breathe out through your mouth as you release them.

Chants

Using a chant can help regulate your breathing and induce a meditative state. You don't have to use 'om', but it does work very well. Start by focusing on your breathing, deep breaths in and deep breaths out then, when you are ready, inhale and on the exhale chant...using 'om' as an example. As you exhale you hold the sounds and syllables of the word om:

Ooooouuuuueeeeemmmmm.

That is difficult to type but hopefully you get the gist. Use whatever word works for you.

The Awen used in druidry works well: 'Aaaaoooooweeeen.' The word you use needs to be soft and have enough syllables to carry you through your exhale. And it is preferable to use a nice positive word too.

Once you are well practised and can hold deeper breaths you can use longer chants. 'Om mani padme hum' is a lovely Tibetan chant, the Sanskrit roughly translates as 'om' – the pure body, speech and mind of Buddha and Bodhisattva, 'mani' meaning the jewel, which symbolises the method, compassion and joy; 'padme' or 'peme' referring to the lotus flower that means wisdom and 'hum' indicating union. The chant in total means that through following your path that is union of love and compassion with wisdom you can transform yourself.

'Sabbe sattā sukhi hontu' is a Pali phrase that translates as, 'May all beings be happy.'

'Om shanti shanti shanti' is a Hindu mantra that literally means 'peace' and is sometimes used at the end of Buddhist ceremonies.

Another one to try is 'Ham-sah'; a self-affirming Hindu chant meaning, 'I am that.' Or if you feel in need how about the

Hawaiian prayer 'Ho'oponopono', which asks for reconciliation and forgiveness. (That one may take some practise to actually pronounce it first.)

If you can remember all the syllables, another chant to work with honours Tara, a tantric meditation deity. (She has many other forms as well.) Her chant is: 'OA tāre tuttāre ture svāhā.' 'Om' represents Tara's enlightened body, speech and mind, 'tare' liberates from all discontent, 'tuttare' liberates from fear, 'ture' liberates from duality and 'svaha' or 'soha' means, 'May the meaning of the mantra take root in my mind.'

But...you don't have to chant a mantra in a different language. You can make up your own, something that is personal to you, maybe 'I am worthy' or 'I can change my world' or even just chanting something simple like 'Peace'.

Sound

Some people like the sound of silence when they meditate and it can work very well. I also like to sit in the garden (or field or forest) to meditate too, so that the only sounds I can hear are the birds and the trees.

However, I also love to meditate to the sound of a drum beat, either creating the drum beat myself or via electronic means. I have a beautiful stag skin drum that has a gorgeous sound, but I also use my mobile phone as there are plenty of drum beat/shamanic beat apps and YouTube can also provide some very good drum soundtracks. You don't need an expensive drum, try using an old biscuit tin or release your inner child and hit a saucepan with a wooden spoon! How slow or fast the drum beat is will be a personal thing, go with what works for you, but you will also find that the speed of the drum beat will also affect the sort of meditation you have. I find that a slower beat provides a more relaxing and insightful meditation experience, but a faster beat often brings very shamanic images of wild animals and primeval visions.

Singing bowls also provide a very good sound backdrop for meditation, but from personal experience you will need to find one that resonates with you. Some of them set my teeth on edge, which is not in the least bit relaxing. So it may be trial and error to find one that suits you. Again check out phone apps and YouTube if you don't own a singing bowl.

Music also works very well and it will depend on your own personal choice as to whether you go for something light such as piano, flute or harp music or you may prefer a voice singing, perhaps Celtic or folk music. You might also like to work with Hindu or Buddhist chants. All of these can be found on YouTube or CDs.

Nature sounds are lovely to work with and if you don't

actually have a large scenic waterfall in your back garden then look again to phone apps, CDs and YouTube as there are lots of different options from waterfalls to forest sounds to rain or the ocean, all of which can be incredibly soothing and hypnotic.

Even something as simple as a loud ticking clock or a metronome can also aid your meditation. Experiment and find out what works for you. You may also find that different sounds suit particular types and purposes of meditation. I use drumming when I want to journey and occasionally when I hedge ride, but if I want something relaxing I often listen to Hindu chants. But just sitting listening to the sounds in the garden, the birds, the neighbour mowing his lawn and the children across the way laughing can also be hypnotic.

Visualisation

Good visualisation will also help with your meditation experience. Being able to see images and focus on them in your head really helps, but don't worry if it doesn't happen at first. Like everything worthwhile it takes practise; here is an exercise to help with your visualisation skills:

Make yourself comfortable in a quiet place where you won't be disturbed.

Close your eyes and focus on your breathing, taking in white cleansing light as you breathe in and letting out all your worries and stresses as you breathe out.

When you are calm and peaceful, focus on your third eye (that's the spot between your eyebrows).

Visualise the image of a round and shiny hazelnut.

In your visualisation turn the hazelnut round and upside down, really examine it and all its details.

If you feel your mind starting to wander or get distracted, bring your focus back to the nut.

Focus on the hazelnut and visualise a tiny shoot cracking through the shell and starting to grow.

Then a tiny root.

Watch the shoot grow and produce leaves, then branches.

Watch the root grow and divide and multiply.

Watch buds form on the branches.

Watch them transform into seeds and grow into plump round hazelnuts.

Reach out and pluck a nut from the tree.

Crack it open – hear the sound of the shell breaking.

Pop the hazelnut into your mouth and eat it.

Really taste it and savour the flavour and texture.

Take a moment to focus on your experience then gradually come back to the present, stretch your arms and legs.

This exercise is a good one to do regularly when you are first learning as it helps you to focus, to have a clear mind and to visualise.

Memory Game

Do you remember playing the memory game as a child? It works really well to 'train' your mind and to help with your visualisation skills.

Lay several objects on a tray, just normal household ones such as a tea cup, keys, a vase, notebook, purse, fork, pretty much anything you have to hand. Then sit quietly and memorise each item, taking in all the details for each one. Now cover the items with a cloth (towel or a tea towel) and see how many of the items you can recall and how much of the detail for each one. Visualise them in your mind's eye, recreating each image in as much detail as possible. You win chocolate for each one you can remember...

Meditation Tea Blends

I find it best to meditate on an empty stomach or when I haven't eaten too much, attempting to meditate after a huge dinner just makes me sleepy...

Drinking a special tea blend before you start your meditation can help you focus. Here are some ideas to get you started, but experiment with the herbs and spices you have in your kitchen cupboards, see what works for you. Herbal tea can sometimes be a bit bland or bitter; if you find it so just add a teaspoon of honey or sugar. But please be careful if you are pregnant or taking any kind of medication, check with a qualified practitioner first. Herbal remedies and teas can have adverse affects when taken with some medications and some can be dangerous for pregnant ladies.

Here are some suggested herbs that could be used for meditative, calming and relaxing effects. They all have lots of different magical properties, but I have listed the ones that should specifically help with meditation:

Basil – Love, happiness and peace.
Caraway – Health, memory and love.
Cardamom – Love, clarity and uplifting.
Chamomile – Sleep, dreams, love, calming, relaxing, purifying and balancing.
Chrysanthemum – Spirituality.
Cinnamon – Healing, psychic powers, love, focus and spirituality.
Cloves – Love and commitment.
Cocoa nibs – Happiness, love and positive energy.
Coriander – Healing, peace, love and release.
Elderflower – Healing, intuition and rebirth.
Ginger – Love, healing and cleansing.
Jasmine petals – Dreams, love and meditation.

Juniper – Love, healing, purification, psychic powers and clarity.

Lavender – Happiness, peace, love, sleep and clarity.

Lemon – Purification, happiness, decisions, uplifting and love.

Lemon balm – Healing, memory and love.

Lemon verbena – Purification and love.

Lemongrass – Happiness, knowledge and shape shifting.

Liquorice – Love and balance.

Mallow flowers – Love

Marigold – Psychic powers, dreams and happiness.

Mugwort – Psychic powers, dreams, healing, cleansing and astral travel.

Orange – Love, happiness, uplifting, purification and clarity.

Peppermint – Healing, cleansing and calming.

Rose petals and rose hips – Love, psychic powers, healing, peace, knowledge and dream help.

Rosemary – Love, mental powers, purification, healing and sleep.

Saffron – Happiness, healing and psychic powers.

Skullcap – De-stress and peace.

Star anise – Psychic powers, purification, dreams, sleep and spirituality.

Green or black tea – Meditation.

You don't need to source herbs and flowers of course, you can use ready-made herbal teabags on their own or mix them up to create your own blends. Liquorice and peppermint together is one of my own personal favourites. If you have home-grown herbs and flowers then fantastic, but if you don't and there is an Asian supermarket near you they are brilliant for sourcing very inexpensive herbs and spices. Otherwise, just take a look in your local market, farmers' market or supermarket.

For all of the following recipes add your ingredients to a cup of boiling water and allow them to steep for 3-5 minutes then strain.

Meditation Tea #1
Two slices of root ginger
Two slices of lemon
½ teaspoon lavender flowers

Meditation Tea #2
2 teaspoons dried peppermint or a bunch of fresh leaves
3 or 4 rose petals
2 saffron stamens

Meditation Tea #3
1 tablespoon green tea
3 or 4 rose petals
1 pinch skullcap

Meditation Tea #4
2 teaspoons chamomile flowers
1 teaspoon honey

Meditation Tea #5
1 cardamom pod
1 clove
½ star anise
¼ teaspoon ground cinnamon
2 teaspoons black or green tea

Meditation Tea #6
1 teaspoon dried peppermint
1 teaspoon chamomile flowers

Meditation Tea #7
1 teaspoon dried peppermint
½ teaspoon dried liquorice

Meditation Incense Blends

If I am sitting down for a long meditation session, or with a specific meditation journey in mind, I often make a loose incense blend to burn to help me. There are lots of lovely incense ingredients that are good for incense blends. I have listed some suggestions below, but go with what works for you and experiment with your own blends. Ingredients don't need to be expensive either; as I mentioned above in herbal teas, there are lots of places to source them cheaply. You don't need to use fancy ingredients, pretty much all herbs and spices burn well as do dried flower heads. I believe in using what I have to hand and not spending huge amounts of money sourcing a rare organic root from the other side of the planet when I have a cupboard full of herbs and spices that cost me very little. Just test them first because not all herbs, spices, roots and flowers actually smell nice once they hit the charcoal...

In addition to the tea blend herbs suggested above, all of which can be used in incense blends, here are some more suggested herbs and plants to use in meditation incense blends:

Benzoin – Calm, purification and love.
Frankincense – Purification, spirituality, relaxation, focus and love.
Honeysuckle – Psychic powers, balance, memory and meditation.
Mace – Purification and psychic powers.
Meadowsweet – Peace, happiness and love.
Myrrh – Purification, healing and the Underworld.
Passion flower – Love, calm, peace and sleep.
Patchouli – Grounding, balance and calm.
Pennyroyal – Peace.
Sage – Wisdom, purification, stimulation and intuition.

Red sandalwood – Meditation and love.

White sandalwood – Purification and psychic powers.

Thyme – Healing, peace, psychic powers, love, purification, sleep and release.

Vervain – Love, purification, peace, sleep, inspiration and shape shifting.

Violet – Love, peace, healing and rebirth.

Yarrow – Psychic powers, love, dreams, peace and happiness.

When I create a loose incense blend I always start with a resin as this helps the mix to burn for longer and also add in something woody, again to help it burn for longer. If you just chuck a handful of dried herbs onto a charcoal disc it will be burnt out in seconds. Be warned though...resin especially makes a lot of smoke! It is personal preference as to whether you keep the herbs, spices and resins whole or slightly crushed or if you prefer to grind them to a powder in a pestle and mortar (or the end of a rolling pin in a small bowl). Don't forget that you can use the stalks of the herbs as well, rosemary especially is very woody, so it helps the incense blend to burn for longer.

You can also theme your incense blends. If the intention of your meditation is to connect with a certain deity, totem animal or place you can tailor the ingredients to suit.

Meditation Incense #1
3 parts benzoin
2 parts lavender
1 pinch mugwort

Meditation Incense #2
3 parts sandalwood
3 parts benzoin
1 part mugwort

Meditation Incense #3
2 parts sandalwood
1 part dried orange peel
1 part mace
1 part cinnamon

Meditation Incense #4
2 parts sandalwood
1 part rose petals
1 part myrrh
1 part jasmine

Meditation Incense #5
2 parts frankincense
2 parts juniper
1 part sandalwood
1 part cinnamon
3 drops patchouli oil

Meditation Incense #6
2 parts copal
1 part jasmine
1 part chamomile
1 part passion flower
1 part lavender

Meditation Incense #7
2 parts frankincense
1 part clove
1 part orange peel
1 part lavender

Meditation Incense #8
1 part frankincense
1 part rosemary
1 part sage
1 part cinnamon

Meditating with Crystals

You can use crystals as an aid to meditation by just holding one or two in your hand or placing one on your altar and if you are lying down you can balance a crystal on your heart or third eye chakra. But you can also journey with and into the crystals themselves.

Blue coloured calming stones, such as aquamarine, blue calcite and turquoise, will help to clear your mind and bring about a feeling of calm to your body.

Purple and clear stones, such as amethyst, clear quartz and charoite, can help you to reach a higher state of consciousness.

Most healing stones are useful to use during meditation, such as agate, amethyst, amazonite, ametrine, aquamarine, aventurine, carnelian, citrine, chrysoprase, quartz, Herkimer diamond, moonstone, bloodstone, amber, snowflake obsidian and jet.

I have listed here some crystal suggestions. They obviously have lots of different magical and specific healing properties associated with them, but I have given the uses relevant to meditation:

Agate (banded) – A good balancing stone and a good all healer, it also improves memory and concentration.

Amber – A good stone for self healing, it also improves memory and relieves depression. It is a good stone to focus on for past life work and astral travel, also for increasing your psychic abilities.

Amethyst – An all-round healing stone for the mind, emotions, body and spirit. It is a powerful psychic enhancer and can restore energies.

Ametrine – Cleansing and balancing, this stone fills the body with light. It is a good stone to work with for spirit, power animal or angel contacts. It also helps with astral projection and offers a doorway into other realms.

Apophyllite – Brings mental clarity, good memory and concentration. It helps you prioritise and fine tune, and is very good for deep meditation, astral projection, past life recall, remembering your dreams and clairvoyance.

Aquamarine – Increases intuition, psychic awareness and clairvoyance and is an excellent focus for meditation and visualization especially for lost worlds such as Atlantis and Lemuria.

Aventurine (green) – Enhances mental perception and brings a calming energy. It is useful to induce psychic dreams and for clairvoyance.

Bloodstone – A good past life stone.

Blue calcite – Brilliant for meditation and instigating creative dreams.

Blue lace agate – Calming and stress relieving, this stone also brings renewed energy for healing others. It is a crystal of peace. It also helps develop clairaudience skills.

Carnelian – A good past life crystal and also helps with psychic protection.

Charoite – Helps with sleep, an excellent past life crystal to work with and can help with telepathic abilities.

Chrysocolla – A healing, peaceful stone that can help induce psychic dreams and bring answers to you.

Chrysoprase – A lovely healing stone that makes the mind, body and spirit receptive to healing energies. It is excellent for meditation, especially when you are outside and want help to connect with the energies of nature.

Citrine – A stone for easing depression and helping bring clarity of thought. Citrine enhances your intuition and helps unlock your inner voice. It is also a useful stone to use in creative visualization to help bring your goals into reality.

Clear quartz – An incredibly versatile crystal for all kinds of uses, it absorbs negative energy and transforms it into healing and positive vibes. Quartz amplifies your psychic and healing abilities and can act as a channel for spirit and animal guides or angels.

Fuchsite – A stone of inspired thinking and a good crystal to use for astral projection or spirit guide contact. It also works well as a connection to the Faerie world.

Hematite – A good stone for self healing and balance, it also works well for astral travel as it provides grounding and protection alongside stimulating your astral connections.

Herkimer diamond – This stone works on the deepest levels allowing spiritual healing and the opening of your chakras and aura. It helps with spiritual dreams and dream recall and helps with astral travel. It also aids in visualization skills.

Jade – Boosts self healing and brings calm and balance to the mind and emotions. It also aids with self love and self esteem.

Jet – Can be used as a doorway into other realms and makes an excellent past life stone.

Kunzite – An excellent stone to develop your intuition and helps in spirit and animal guide, nature spirit and angel contact.

Labradorite – Brings creative dreams and helps with psychic abilities.

Larimar – A self healing stone and helpful to de-stress. It also hones your telepathic abilities and aids in working with the Akashic Records.

Merlinite – A shamanic type stone that allows you to communicate with the elementals and the energy of nature. It gives you access to your deepest intuition and helps give contact with spirit guides. It is also a stone of harmony that helps give clear psychic visions.

Moonstone – A very magical stone, this works well in developing psychic abilities and channelling messages.

Moss agate – Use a clear moss agate stone as a gateway during meditation to lead you into other realms.

Muscovite – Increases spiritual growth and aids with psychic abilities.

Orange calcite – A good crystal for relaxation and to help enhance your intuition.

Peridot – A stone that fills your mind, body and spirit with a sense of peace and general well-being.

Petallite – Increases your awareness and helps you connect with the spirit world and other realms.

Prehnite – A balancing and healing stone that helps with dream recall.

Rhodochrosite – A strong healing stone, especially on an emotional level.

Rhodonite – A good healing stone, particularly on a mental level, allowing you to let go.

Rose quartz – A good all-round healing stone not just on a physical level, but also for emotional grief, stress, anger and fear. It is a beautiful stone of peace and works well for psychic work.

Sapphire – A spiritual healing stone. Particularly good for channelling work, it is also good for assisting with clairvoyance and clairaudience and helps boost your psychic powers.

Selenite – A very strong crystal to use for psychic connections, it works with the spirit world, angels and ancestors and assists with dream recollection and any past life work.

Serpentine – A balancing and calming stone, it also helps with visualization skills.

Snowflake obsidian – Excellent to place on your third eye during meditation, it is soothing and calming and will help with spirit world connection.

Sugilite – A stone that was made for meditation. It helps open the channels and bring awareness of other realms.

Tanzanite – Helps connect you to ancient wisdom and other spiritual realms.

Turquoise – A spiritual stone that helps open the door to the Akashic Records and all the wisdom of the world.

Variscite – Calming and balancing, this is an excellent stone to use for channelling, contacting the Akashic Records, journeying and vision quests.

When you meditate with a crystal for a particular purpose, for healing yourself, connecting with a particular element (earth, air, fire, water) or perhaps a specific angel or deity, select a crystal that you feel associates with your intent. You can then either hold the crystal in your hand or set it in front of you.

You will need to connect with the energy of that crystal, visualize the energy radiating from the crystal and connecting with you.

You can also pack your virtual rucksack and pop on your imaginary hiking boots and take a trip into a crystal. This works best with larger crystals that have inclusions (imperfections) and lots of facets. Visualise yourself shrinking down *Alice in Wonderland* style so that you are small enough to scale the heights of the crystal, hike up the slopes, investigate the valleys, dips and peaks and see where it takes you. Remember to come back to full size afterwards…

Crystal meditation also works well for past life exploration. Find a crystal for that specific purpose, one that feels right to you, but some suggestions are variscite, quartz, tanzanite, prehnite, lepidolite, merlinite, peridot, amber, carnelian, garnet, serpentine and green aventurine. Large cloudy crystals work well. Place the crystal in front of you and visualize a doorway appearing in the side of the crystal. Connect with the energy of the crystal then walk through the doorway…see where (and when) it takes you… To return to reality, just count slowly backwards from ten to one.

Crystal Meditation

Lay on the floor or your bed.

Use whatever crystals your intuition guides you to.

You will need at least eight crystals for this meditation, it doesn't matter what size or colour.

Start by placing one crystal just above where your head will be when you lie down, with another by your feet. Then put one where you will be able to reach it on your left side and another on your right side.

Hold the remaining crystals in your hand, lie down. Place one crystal on your forehead in the position of your third eye. Place another on your throat. Then put one on your heart and another on your solar plexus. Then pick up the crystals that are on either side of you and hold them while you meditate. Balancing these crystals on your body may be a bit tricky; you may have to be ingenious!

Close your eyes and begin to focus on your breathing. Once you are calm and relaxed, focus your attention on the crystal above your head. See the crystal filled with light that flows from the crystal down through your head and into the crystal on your third eye; see that crystal then fill with bright, positive light and allow that to travel to the next crystal. Keep doing this until all the crystals are linked via your body by bright, positive light. Notice what colour each crystal sends out and be aware of any areas of your body that the crystal energy may seem sluggish on.

At this point you may allow your mind to open to see what comes, it may be a spirit guide, it may be clarity on an issue you have, it could be anything – see what happens.

When you are ready, visualise all the positive energy being locked into your body, then visualise the light forming a protective cloak around you.

Finally bring yourself slowly back.

When you are ready, stretch your arms and legs and slowly stand up.

Pathworking

Sometimes called journeying, inner plane work or vision questing, pathworking is a form of meditation used a lot in shamanic practice. It is a structured meditation with a purpose to it, a guided journey into our inner world or onto other planes or other worlds such as the Otherworld or into the land of Fae. It is a practice that should only be undertaken by those more experienced in meditation skills.

This type of journeying allows us to stretch ourselves, to dip into our inner power, to connect with divinity, to aid us in decision-making, to seek out past lives and to connect with messengers and guides.

Pathworking allows us to go beyond our conscious mind and even our universe because it creates a link between our conscious and subconscious minds, allowing us to access memories and psychic skills we may not usually reach. It will also have lasting effects. Once you have pathworked and connected with those guides or powers it will become apparent in your everyday life.

Once you have gained the skill for pathworking successfully, you will be able to wander freely and safely within all the inner realms and connect with the divine to gain insight, to explore new ideas, to meet new guides and to expand your entire potential.

Here are the basics of setting up a pathworking.

Decide what you need from this trip, why are you journeying? What path will you take? What is your destination? What or who would you like to encounter? Obviously you will probably encounter some things you didn't plan for, but that makes it even more worthwhile! What image do you want to use to take you from this world onto your journey? (For example, a gate, a knothole in a tree, a doorway etc).

When you have decided upon those details, you need a framework – starting with an induction. This is where you enter the pathworking, the trance-like state. Then you focus on the body of the pathworking; this is whatever you need to do while in your pathworking, the reason you are there. And then the closure, where you leave the pathworking and come back to reality. The induction and the closure will be pretty close to your 'script', but the body may take different twists and turns other than those you expected.

It helps to write down your framework. I prefer to then record it to my phone or laptop so that I can listen to it, but go with what works for you.

The basic steps for pathworking are very similar to those of meditation:

1. Find a safe, quiet and comfortable place. Make sure you won't be disturbed.
2. Ground and centre.
3. Turn on your recording or just close your eyes to begin your journey. Visualise your induction point, the entry to your journey. Just listening to or visualising your induction should take you into your trance state, but if it doesn't focus on your breathing to obtain a meditative state.
4. Visualise your induction, see yourself at the entry. Take a moment to fix that place in your mind. See yourself reaching out to touch the entry way. Feel how real it is, notice all the details, the feel, any sounds, any smells.
5. Once you have the entry point in your mind solidly you can begin your journey.
6. Walking through the gateway, enter the body of your journey, notice all the details – listen, touch, smell, hear, taste, take note of everything. Set the details in your mind so that you will recall them when you come back to reality. Sometimes even the smallest detail may be important.

7. If you meet anyone on your pathworking whether it be a human, a deity, a faery, an animal, whatever it is, please be polite and respectful. Don't touch any animal or being without asking first. If you are asked to move on then do so with respect. These beings work on a different plane, you do not want to upset them. Do not take anything unless you know it has actually been given to you. Use your common sense and mind your manners.

8. When you have finished your pathworking return to the point you started at. Go back to your gateway and go through, but do so slowly, coming back to reality gently and calmly.

9. Always ground afterwards.

A traditional use of pathworking is to connect with the elements and the deities and elementals that work within those realms.

So let's start with a basic framework.

Decide what you want to use as your gateway – it might be an old oak door, it might be a gap between the roots of a large oak tree, a doorway into the clouds, a stairway, a rose arch in a stone wall – it's your gateway you decide. It helps to have a short pathway that leads up to your gateway so that you have time to get into a meditative state; use the same gateway and same pathway each time you journey.

Okay, so if you were to journey to the element of earth what would you visualise? You need to decide what environment makes you think of the element of earth, is it rocks? Desert? A dense forest? Get a picture of it in your mind, make some notes on what you want to visualise. Think about what scents there would be too. But bear in mind that this might change depending on where your subconscious takes you...

For this example our intention is to meet the elemental guardian of that realm, so at some point in your pathworking you need to figure in meeting that entity.

If you have any questions for that elemental guardian have a think about them before you start.

And then plan a pathway back to your gateway to return.

To follow, you could put together a pathworking for the other elements: air, fire and water.

I am deliberately leaving these instructions vague as it is your journey and therefore up to you to put all the details together. Each one will start at your gateway; each one will have the purpose of experiencing each element and meeting the elemental guardian for that element.

Once you have put all the details together you will have outlines for four separate pathworkings.

This is just an example of what journeys you can take with pathworking, but the subject and destinations are really up to you. It could be that you need a specific question answered or you want to connect with a deity or animal guide, so you would tailor your pathworking plan of action to your intent.

Shape Shifting

Although perhaps not technically meditation, for shape shifting you do need to be in that same meditative frame of mind and it is an amazing experience. It is a huge subject of which I am only giving a brief outline here, but if it interests you I would encourage you to explore further.

Shape shifting can help you understand people and behaviour, whether it is at home or at work. It can give you strength and courage and help you achieve your goals. It can help you adapt to different situations and open up your creative abilities. Shape shifting can help you develop discipline and bring about transformation and it can also help hone your intuition and observation skills. It can also aid with your spirit contact, astral travel and lucid dreaming and give you a deeper connection to your animal totem.

I would first say...don't take on the exercise of shape shifting until you have at least some experience with meditation, it can be very overwhelming. And make sure you do some research first, for example a vegetarian may not want to shape shift into a lion...because it could leave you with an sudden urge for beef burgers (or zebra)...basically start small and start with a gentle type of animal.

Shape shifting is all about changing, morphing into your chosen animal – not just turning your arms into wings or your feet into paws, but also getting into the character and personality of that animal.

I find that the best way to work a shape shifting is to have a photograph of the animal in front of me when I start. You will need to do some research so that you know what type of habitat the animal lives in.

Shape Shifting Meditation

Make yourself comfortable, light some incense and play some peaceful music if you wish.

Close your eyes and focus on your breathing, deep breaths in and deep breaths out.

As your world around you dissipates you find yourself in (insert the habitat of the animal that you wish to seek whether it is a desert, a forest, the bank of a stream etc). Just ahead of you stands a full length mirror. It is beautiful and sparkles in the light.

Walk towards the mirror and as you do so you notice that it reflects your entire surroundings back at you and then starts to fill with a swirling mist. Once you are standing right in front of the mirror the mists start to clear and you see the image of an animal gazing back at you. This creature can teach you, it can guide you. To connect and shape shift into this animal all you need to do is step through the mirror.

Allow yourself to become that animal, watch as each part of your outer body changes. Once you have become that animal, walk around your surroundings. See how they see, smell what they smell, feel what they feel, and test out your new animal frame. Explore and see what challenges you meet and how the animal deals with them. Take note of this...

Once you have completed your journey return to the mirror and step back through, as you do so your body slowly changes back. Walk away from the mirror and make sure you are feeling completely human again...and when you are ready open your eyes.

Remember or write down your experiences and how you felt. You can refer back to this experience and even call upon some of the energies of that animal when you need them in your real life.

Hedge Riding

A hedge witch has one foot in this world and the other in the Underworld. Hedge riding is the term used to describe the journeys that a hedge witch makes, very similar in fact to the Underworld/Otherworld journeys that a shamanic practitioner makes. Again I won't go into too much detail on this as there are some good books out there that will help you further if you are interested, but it is another meditation practice that requires some experience.

The hedge is the symbolic boundary between the worlds. Hedge riding is the journey your spirit takes into the Otherworld or Underworld realms, sometimes called the upper and lower realms. The middle realm is our everyday world that we live in.

Hedge riding can take our spirit travelling back into the past to connect with our ancestors. We can meet and talk with our past life selves. The upper realm can provide us with connections to our spirit guides and teachers and the Divine. The lower realm takes us on a journey to find animal guides and to meet the souls of those passed over.

Hedge riding is not something to be taken lightly, it definitely isn't somewhere to just visit because you are bored, it is something to be taken very seriously and journeys should be taken with a particular question or mission in mind. It might be a journey undertaken for the purposes of healing, seeking an answer to a question, for spell work or to find spiritual enlightenment.

Personally I would advise becoming experienced in pathworking, shape shifting and astral travel before attempting to hedge ride, not purely for safety, but also because it will help you with the journey. This is not something to be attempted by those just stepping onto the meditation ladder. Hedge riding should also be avoided if you are feeling unwell or if you have any kind of mental illness.

Hedge riding is very similar to shamanic journeys and also incorporates the art of seidh or 'seer work' in that you will communicate with the spirits. Shamanic work often involves soul retrieval. This is something that doesn't usually occur with hedge riding and is probably something best left to trained shamans.

During a journey your spirit, your consciousness, will travel to the Otherworld and while there you will need to take note of any symbols or signs that you see and any sounds you hear or scents you smell as they may all be important.

A hedge witch will enter the Otherworld via a trance state, an altered state of conscious when your mind and spirit work separately from your physical body. You are not fully conscious, but you are not unconscious. You are in that wonderful state in between, but you are always fully aware of what you are doing. You are lucid and in control, but don't fall asleep.

Altered states of consciousness can be induced via means of drugs, but I would wholeheartedly NOT advise this route. You will need to go past the state of meditation and on to pathworking to achieve hedge riding. I find drumming helps, but chanting can also be very useful. Shamanic music with drums and rattles is also good; any rhythmic beat will work well.

Keep a notebook with you when you hedge ride, then you can jot down anything that you saw or heard as soon as you come back to reality because it has a habit of slipping away once you get up and move about. I recommend writing down absolutely everything, even the small details.

Hedge riding equipment – well you don't *need* anything, just your mind, but you can use a few bits and bobs to help your journey along.

Rattles and drums can be used to get you into a trance state as I have mentioned above, but they can also help to clear away any negative energy, call to the spirit guides and help bring in healing energies. I would also advise smudging your room before you begin any journey.

Many hedge witches (and shamans) have a medicine bag that they use to keep magical items in to aid in journeying. Each bag will be personal and specific to each individual. It might contain beads, shells, feathers, pebbles, herbs and crystals. If you decide to make your own bag, be guided by your intuition and add whatever you feel is necessary to help you on your hedge riding.

Ointments – you have all probably read or heard about flying ointments, these did actually exist and were usually made from all sorts of nasty and quite often fatal ingredients, and personally I would avoid these as it is really not worth taking a chance. Instead of an ointment you can use incense blended with herbs and natural items that correspond to contacting the spirit world, Otherworld and to aid in psychic abilities.

An animal spirit guide is extremely useful to journey to the other side of the hedge with. In my experience you don't choose your animal guide, it chooses you. Don't be surprised if your hedge riding guide is a different one from your usual power animal and you may also find that your guide to the different worlds will be different in each one and they might even be different for each journey you take or you may have the same guide every time...be open to whatever you meet.

You might find that it takes a few hedge riding journeys before you meet any spirit guides and you may find different guides in each world. They may be there to guide you, they may be there to give you a message, but it won't always be via spoken word; look out for signs and symbols.

The Three Realms

So let's talk about the three realms that a hedge witch can enter...and I am going to describe the general ideas, but...your experience may be different.

Generally (not always) a hedge witch will access the worlds via a tree, often it is seen as the Tree of Life and it is a portal to the Otherworld. You might see an entrance between the roots, which takes you to the lower world, there might be an entrance halfway up the trunk to the middle world and an entrance in the upper branches to the upper world – what you see might be different. There is also another level accessed via the lower world, this takes you down another level to the Underworld. How you see it might be different to this description, you might access all worlds via the same tunnel that splits in different directions or you might access it through another portal other than a tree...

The Underworld/Hades/Tir na n-Og/Helheim

The Underworld, or the lower world as it is sometimes called, is not a deep, dark fiery hell pit...really it isn't. It can, however, be seen as darker than the middle world. It may often appear as a cave or a very primordial jungle. You can find dangers in the Underworld, but you can also meet them in the middle and upper world too. The Underworld is earthy, stable and grounding, it is the base from which the world grows. The Underworld deals with emotions, our intuition and our very basic needs. You may meet ancestors here; animal guides, guardians, plant spirits and the Underworld Kings and Queens along with the Faerie realm are found here. If you are experienced in hedge riding this is also the place to do soul retrieval.

The Middle World/Earth/Midgard/Bith

The middle world is often used as a place for time travel. (You are now thinking Doctor Who and his Tardis aren't you?) The middle world is very much like our own and you can find yourself in any familiar type of structure, building or landscape. This world is as much full of bad spirits as it is good, so be wary. You will find earth and fertility deities here along with the elementals, land guardian spirits, messenger deities, nature spirits and the Wild Hunt.

The Upper World/Avalon/Asgard/Olympus
This world is beeeeautiful. Spirits live here and it shows. Think beautiful landscapes, dreamy clouds, sparkling streams and all that is amazing. This is the place to meet and greet spirit guides, angels, ascended masters, devas, deities and animal guides. It is the upper astral, the spiritual plane and a place of enlightenment. This world will show you knowledge, inspiration, ideas and wisdom (hopefully) and also provide healing. The upper world can also help you remove yourself from your ego and see things as they really are.

For your Ride

You may want to cast a circle before you journey. I don't, but it is your personal choice. You may prefer to just cast a personal 'shield' of protective light around yourself before you start. My home has plenty of protection in and around it already. Make sure you are comfortable, and remember that sitting still for any period of time lowers your body temperature so you might want a shawl or a blanket to hand. I like to smudge the room first and light some incense, I also prefer the lighting low and some candle light. You may want to sit and hold your medicine pouch if you have one or a crystal to help focus you. I also like to play a CD with shamanic drumming or singing bowls to help alter my conscious.

Don't forget it is very wise to ground and centre before *and* after any journeying.

Before you start your hedge ride, make sure you have an idea of what your purpose and intent is, whether it is a question you need an answer to, advice on a situation or healing and throughout your journey keep focused on your intent.

If you are looking for answers, take note of any symbols you see, objects you find, people or animals you meet. You may also come across pools of water that can be used for scrying.

Healing can be achieved by bathing in oceans, streams or

pools or you can use the energy from your animal guides to help the healing process. Your guides can also help with protection requirements.

Your spirit guides in the upper world can help you out if you are seeking knowledge.

Please remember to always be polite and courteous to any animal or being that you meet in any of the worlds – treat them with respect at all times.

If you should meet any spirit that you don't like, politely but firmly ask them to leave – you have the power to make it leave…you are in control at all times.

Astral Travel

Astral travel is sometimes called astral journeying, astral projection or an out-of-body experience. It means that the part of you, your true inner self, leaves your physical body and travels to another reality or another place.

Every living thing has an etheric counterpart. The lower etheric plane is quite a dangerous place. If you find yourself there during an out-of-body experience it is recommended to quickly raise your vibrations and change your trip by looking upwards to find a better level, it may be signified by a bright white light or lots of bright colours.

The higher etheric plane, sometimes called the high astral or spiritual plane, is a very spiritual place. This is where you will find incredibly wonderful spiritual beings.

I believe that there are many, many etheric planes in between the higher and the lower planes.

The astral plane itself is a very emotional place. We are, after all, sending our astral self there, which is full of emotions. Hopefully your astral experiences will be wonderful and interesting, but please beware that sometimes they can be a bit scary and occasionally unpleasant. It is our own level of vibrations that determine which level of plane we visit. Remember *you* are always in control.

So why would you want to astral travel? Well, it is a good way of visiting those who have passed on. It is also a way of travelling to interesting places, to learn, to experience, to gain knowledge and insight. And, of course, the astral plane isn't restricted by time or dimension…

As I mentioned before, astral travel can be difficult, it can take some time to master. It does take practise. We can leave our physical body once we are in a very relaxed state, that moment just between sleeping and waking.

There are various methods for performing astral travel. Below are some ideas. To start with, determine a location that you want to visit astrally. Sit in a comfortable position, somewhere quiet where you will not be disturbed. Focus on your breathing.

Method 1

When you are in a calm, centred and relaxed state, try to separate your astral body from your physical body, starting by visualising it floating a foot or so above your physical body. Then you can send your astral body to wherever you want to, visualise your destination and send your body there.

Method 2

Another method is to expand your body roughly half an inch with each breath. This is done only with visualisation, is fairly easy to do, and often produces fast results.

When you have expanded to roughly twice your normal size, continue the process with even greater dimensions. Inches become feet, and feet become miles, and so on. Don't worry too much about the actual act of leaving your body.

One variation of this technique consists of proceeding little by little. For example, the first few times you would only move your astral arms out of your physical body, a bit later your whole upper body and head, and so on. Always keep in mind that obtaining the remote information is your actual goal, regardless of how you get there, and not necessarily the act of buzzing around in an astral body.

Method 3

Start with the basics, using either of the methods above to separate your astral body, but instead of disappearing off to the Bahamas; take an astral walk around your home. Feel your astral body strolling around the rooms in your house and remotely viewing all that they contain.

Method 4: The Lift/Roll-Out Technique

Once you have reached a very deep level of relaxation (trance state), you must then use your powers of visualisation. Simply imagine yourself floating upwards out of your body. Tell yourself all the time how nice it is to do this, how pleasant, how great it would be to be floating out of the body. Continue to image this floating feeling.

It often helps to imagine an aid or accessory to this floating process. For instance, you may imagine hundreds of small birds all flying up and pulling their own little pieces of string, which are all attached to your non-physical body. All the time they are pulling you gently out of the physical body. You can use any adaptation to this – whatever helps you imagine that you are floating up.

As you imagine this you will feel the vibrations beginning – ignore them totally. Simply continue to imagine yourself floating upwards.

After a relatively short while you will feel yourself come free of the physical body. This is often quite a sudden sensation as the non-physical body breaks free of the physical body. Like a piece of rubber being stretched and pulled until all of a sudden one end is let go...

You will then find yourself outside your physical body.

A common variation on this technique is the roll-out method.

This is very similar, except that instead of imagining that you are floating upward, imagine that you are rolling sideways out of your body. Feel yourself gently rocking from side to side. Very slowly at first, but gradually building the momentum until eventually you will reach that critical point where you will actually break free from, and actually roll out of, your physical body.

Method 5: The Anchor Technique

The basis of this method is to focus on an anchor point outside of the physical body. There are two basic variations to this technique

– the fixed anchor, and the moving anchor. As with all the techniques described, a deep level of relaxation is required.

Once you have reached a very deep level of relaxation (trance state), you must then use your powers of visualisation.

The Fixed Anchor

After reaching the trance state, focus on a point outside of the physical body. For example, if you are on your bed focus on the end of it. You can either simply focus on a point in space, or you can imagine an object at that point (it usually helps if it is a familiar object).

Once you can clearly see the focus point in your mind's eye, 'feel' how solid it is. Try pushing it around with your mind, try pulling it, or moving it. The focus point should be totally solid and entirely 'fixed' where it is. No amount of mental manipulation should be able to move it.

Once the focus point is totally fixed, imagine reaching out with your arms and grabbing hold of the focus point. Remember, this *will not move*. Now, try pulling the object towards you, gently at first, and then harder and harder. Gradually as you pull you will feel yourself moving towards the focus point. Finally you will find yourself at the focus point outside your physical body. Congratulations! You have done it!

The Moving Anchor

After reaching the trance state, imagine an object about six feet in front of your eyes, above you. Once again, make this a familiar object. Now, feel this object pulling at you. Once you can see the object clearly in your mind's eye, and feel the pull of the object on you, begin to move the object slowly towards you. Just a small amount at first then, as the object moves towards you, feel the pull getting stronger. Now move it back again. Now repeat the process a few times moving the object closer each time and feeling the pull becoming stronger and stronger as the object comes closer.

Once you are comfortable with the movement of the object, begin the process again, only this time the movement of the object should be a fluid motion, and as the object moves to and fro it should be like a wave. You should also feel this wave on yourself as the pull gets stronger and weaker and stronger again. Finally, as the object reaches you the combination of the wave motion and the pulling strength should pull you out of your physical body.

Then you can explore whatever time or realm you choose, just visualise where and when you want to go...

Returning

Once you want to return your astral body to your physical one, ask for permission first and then slowly reconnect. Take your time doing this as you don't want to leave anything unconnected. That would not be comfortable at all...

Chakras

Energy is in all natural things from pebbles on the beach to the plants and trees around us, including crystals, which all carry their own individual energies. Tied in with energy are your chakras. The study of and working with chakras is a huge and fascinating subject, which I have only touched on ever so slightly here in relation to meditation. If it speaks to you I encourage you to seek out more information.

There are seven main chakras, but a lot more that you can investigate if working with chakras interests you. I like to work with nine chakras, not because I am being awkward, it just works for me.

The word 'chakra' is derived from the Sanskrit word meaning 'wheel'. If we could see the chakras (as many people can) we would see a wheel of energy continuously revolving or rotating. Some perceive chakras as colourful wheels or flowers with a hub in the centre.

The chakras begin at the base of the spine and finish at the top of the head. Though fixed in the central spinal column they are located on both the front and back of the body, and work through it.

Each chakra vibrates or rotates at a different speed. Each chakra is stimulated by its own and complementary colours. These are the generally accepted colours, but if you find yours are different then trust your own intuition. I have also put suggested crystal correspondences as well, but again go with what you are drawn to and what works for you. Each chakra also resonates with different aspects of your persona and character.

The main seven chakras are:

Base – Red
The base chakra helps keep you grounded and centred and is

important for your general health and physical energy this chakra is also your *ooh la la* one, which regulates not only your sex drive, but also your ambition too. It is located at the base of your spine, but I am also of the school of thought that believes this chakra can 'float' anywhere between the base of your spine and your feet. Go with what feels right to you.

Crystals associated with the base chakra are ruby, garnet, bloodstone, red jasper, black tourmaline, obsidian, red aventurine and smoky quartz.

Sacral – Orange

The sacral chakra is associated with emotions, vitality, fertility, reproduction and sexual energy it is also the chakra for relationships and sexuality. It is located just below your belly button.

Crystals associated with the sacral chakra are carnelian, amber, topaz, fire agate, fire opal and orange calcite.

Solar Plexus – Yellow

The solar plexus chakra can be found just above your belly button and is your energy centre, your own personal spot for power, action, empowerment and ego.

Crystals associated with the solar plexus chakra are citrine, topaz, amber, tiger's eye, calcite, jasper and sunstone.

Heart – Green (Sometimes Pink)

Well I think you can probably guess where the heart chakra is located...just in the centre of your chest and unsurprisingly it is associated with matters of the heart, love, compassion and affection.

Crystals associated with the heart chakra are emerald, tourmaline, malachite, jade, aventurine, rose quartz, amazonite and chrysocolla.

Throat – Blue

The throat chakra is...yep you guessed it, at the base of your neck and is associated with communication and creative expression.

Crystals associated with the throat chakra are turquoise, chrysocolla, blue topaz, aquamarine, blue lace agate, blue chalcedony, sodalite and angelite.

Third Eye – Indigo

For the third eye chakra think Cyclops because this one is located just between your eyebrows and it corresponds with your inner vision, psychic abilities, your intuition and imagination.

Crystals associated with the third eye chakra are lapis lazuli, azurite, sodalite, quartz, sapphire, amethyst, charolite, sugilite and lepidolite.

Crown – Violet

And the crown? Yep...at the top of your head where your crown would be if you wore one...maybe you do? This chakra is associated with enlightenment and your connection to the Divine.

Crystals associated with the crown chakra are amethyst, diamond, sugilite, fluorite, quartz, danburite, chalcopyrite, moonstone and selenite.

With the addition of:

Soul Star – White

This one is above your head, just up from the crown chakra, not on your body, but just floating above it and is associated with spiritual cleansing, spiritual energy and healing.

Crystals associated with the soul star chakra are quartz, Herkimer diamond, selenite, kyanite, sugilite, amethyst and charoite.

Earth Star – Brown

This chakra connects you to Mother Earth and helps you stay grounded and focused; it is also important to anchor you physically in this reality. It is another floating one like the soul star except this one is below your body, just a little bit below the soles of your feet.

Crystals associated with the earth star chakra are hematite, black tourmaline, snowflake and black obsidian, Apache tears, black kyanite and smoky quartz.

The size and brightness of the wheels vary with individual development, physical condition, energy levels, disease, or stress.

The energy travels between each chakra along a pathway called a 'meridian'. There are several versions of how the energy moves between each chakra; some see it as working in a continuous circle, the energy flowing from one chakra to another flowing up through the chakras, round and back down. Another version is that the energy flows in a criss-cross system similar to the caduceus symbol going from one to the other crossing over as the snakes do, and another idea is that the energy flows in a spiral up and down linking each chakra.

If the chakras are not balanced, or if the energies are blocked, the basic life force will be slowed down. You may feel listless, tired, out of sorts, or depressed. Not only will physical bodily functions be affected so diseases may manifest, but the thought processes and the mind may also be affected. A negative attitude, fear, doubt, etc may preoccupy you.

A constant balance between the chakras promotes health and a sense of well-being. If the chakras are opened too much, you could literally short circuit with too much universal energy going through the body. If the chakras are closed, this does not allow for the universal energy to flow through properly, which may also lead to illness.

Most of us react to unpleasant experiences by blocking our

feelings and stopping a great deal of our natural energy flow. This affects the maturation and development of the chakras.

Whenever a person blocks whatever experience they are having, in turn they block their chakras, which stop working properly or altogether. When the chakras are functioning normally, each will be open, spinning clockwise to metabolize the particular energies needed from the universal energy field.

As already mentioned any imbalances that exist within any chakra may have profound effects upon either our physical or emotional bodies. You can use visualisation and meditate to work with your chakras; you can also aid this by working with crystals that correspond to each chakra.

Chakra Meditation

Make yourself comfortable. I find that lying on the floor or the bed is easiest. You can also place some crystals around you if you would like to.

Close your eyes and focus on your breathing. As you breathe in visualise a bright, white cleansing and purifying light, as you breathe out send out all the negative energies.

Once you are calm and peaceful visualise a white light above your head, allow this light to flow down into your crown chakra. As it meets your chakra visualise the light turning to a beautiful violet colour. Open your chakra by visualising it as a flower, each petal opening and in the centre a violet spinning ball of energy. As the petals of the crown chakra open it opens your spirituality.

Then allow the light from above your head to travel down further to your third eye chakra. As it meets the chakra the light turns to an indigo blue, the chakra becomes a flower. It starts as a bud and then opens out and blossoms to reveal a spinning ball of indigo light. This also opens your ability for telepathy and clairvoyance.

The light then goes to your throat chakra. As the light meets this one it turns into a beautiful bright blue colour and becomes a flower bud. As the petals open you see inside a ball of swirling blue energy. As this flower chakra blossoms it opens your ability for clairaudience and communication.

The light then moves down further to your heart chakra. As the light meets this chakra it turns to a bright green colour and becomes a flower bud. As the petals open, you see inside a ball of swirling green energy. This opens up your ability to feel, your sensitivity, love and awareness, your psychic power and your understanding.

The light moves on to your solar plexus, as the light meets this chakra it turns to a bright yellow colour. As it touches the chakra it turns into a flower bud. The flower blooms and in the centre is a spinning ball of yellow energy. This is the centre of your power. As the flower blossoms it opens your strength and determination.

The light travels down to your sacral chakra, as the light meets this chakra it turns to a bright orange colour and becomes the bud of a flower. As each petal opens, the flower reveals a ball of orange spinning energy in its centre. As this chakra opens, so does your centre of psychic power and inner being.

Further down the light travels to your base chakra. As the light meets this one it turns to a bright red colour and becomes the roots of a tree. As the roots grow your chakra opens to become a ball of swirling red energy. This chakra opens to reveal your ability to ground and centre and to remain connected to the earth. Visualise these roots travelling down into the earth. As they do so they draw energy up into your body.

Spend a few moments now watching these colours of energy swirl around as they heal, soothe and energise your spiritual and physical body.

Now visualise all of the colours forming together to make a protection shield around you, like a bubble. This shield will protect you from negative energies.

Once this is done, slowly, gradually come back to the present. Stretch your arms and legs and clap your hands. Take some time to do this, don't stand up straight away.

It is usually a good idea to have a cup of tea or eat something after this type of exercise... I advise cake.

Akashic Records

I have mentioned Akashic Records a couple of times so I thought I had better explain the term in case you haven't heard of it. Although not strictly under the heading meditation, it does involve trance work of a kind to gain access to the records, so I will give you a very brief outline, but I would encourage you to investigate further as it is a fascinating practice.

The Akashic Records is a vibrational imprint of everything that has ever happened, is happening and will happen in the future. It is a record of every single person and each physical, mental, spiritual and emotional event. Throughout history it has been referred to as a book, a tablet or a library in another realm that can be accessed for information. The Akashic Records holds a completely documented history of your journey, not just in this life but in your past lives and future lives too. It is not a static record, it grows and evolves.

There are many ways to access the Akashic Records and some people will be more naturally skilled at doing so than others. Essentially the first step involves meditation (see that does make it relevant to this book after all) you can then use remote viewing, channelling or lucid dreaming. An experienced practitioner will be able to tune into your records after asking your permission and give you a reading; it is a very intriguing experience.

Meditation Beads

Your mind can sometimes tend to wander when you are meditating, which leads to a loss of concentration. Meditation beads can act as a kind of 'anchor' or grounding point enabling you to focus better. This can be extremely useful especially if you are feeling tired when you meditate.

Conversely, if your mind is too active and over-energised, meditation beads will prevent you from becoming distracted or day-dreaming. And, because the beads are moved in rhythm with your breathing, it helps you maintain your concentration.

Meditation beads can be used in a number of ways. A popular method is to hang the string between your thumb and your third finger, traditionally in your right hand. Using your middle finger, you rotate the beads one bead at a time towards yourself, each time you repeat the mantra and take a breath.

A variation of this method is to hang the string on your middle finger and rotate the beads one at a time in the same fashion, only this time you use your thumb.

You begin the procedure at the first bead and repeat the process with all of the beads, continuing around the loop until you once again reach the start.

On my meditation beads, each bead signifies a different purpose – as I rotate the bead I say quietly to myself a mantra with that specific intent, for instance when I reach the friends bead I say, 'I give thanks for my wonderful friends,' when I am on the Cailleach bead I say, 'I give blessings and honour the Cailleach for guiding me.'

On my meditation beads, each bead has a plain separator, then:

- Green for abundance
- Grey sparkly one for the Cailleach

- Wooden one for the Green Man
- Elephant image for Ganesha
- Daisy one for my friends
- Brown one for my family
- World one for the universe
- Yellow for enlightenment
- Pink for love
- Black to release negativity
- Light blue for healing
- Orange for success
- Green for my totem frog
- Brown/red for my totem wild boar
- Spiral for spirituality
- Purple for wisdom
- Spiral for balance
- Red for empowering
- Sparkly brown for happiness
- Red for manifesting
- Green for money
- Blue for protection
- Brown for strength
- White for cleansing
- Purple for meditation

You can have different beads for different purposes as I have done, or you can have a string of plain beads all the same colour. It is your choice, use whatever works for you.

The beads don't need to be used solely for meditation, you can use them throughout the day. When you awake hold the beads and run them through your fingers and connect with their energy, this will set you up with positive intentions for the day.

Carry the beads with you in your pocket or bag, take them out during the day to remind you to stay grounded and focused on your tasks. Trust me, I need these all the time for focusing!

Hold the beads when you feel stressed or spacey to help bring you back centred and calm.

Finish your day the way you started by running the beads through your fingers and count your blessings, release the negative points from your day and allow them to be replaced by the positive ones, feel the good energy from the fabulous points of your day wash over you.

Share...make a set of prayer/meditation beads for a friend or loved one.

You also don't need to spend huge amounts of money, there are some beautiful meditation beads out there (often called prayer beads or malas), but you can make them yourself with whatever beads you have. There is no need to create a set of beads using expensive natural stones (although they are beautiful and full of natural energy). If all you have is wooden or plastic beads then use them, raid your children's play box even! The idea of the beads is to use them as a focus, so even if you have a string of dried peas the intention is the same...

Meditations

In this section I would like to share with you some guided meditations. They can be read through, remembered and then used as a loose journey or you could record them and listen to them on your laptop or phone, whichever works best for you.

Sacred Space Meditation

Make yourself comfortable and relax.

Close your eyes and focus on your breathing, deep breaths in and deep breaths out.

As your world around you dissipates you find yourself in a place that feels very comfortable to you. It might be a room in a house or perhaps a castle even, it may be a spot in nature, in the woods or on the beach, but you know that it is your own personal space.

Look around you, walk around and see what is in your space...

If you feel it needs something added, maybe some furniture, divination tools or decoration of some sort, then know that you can add it just with a thought...

What is the temperature like? Is it warm enough or cool enough? You can make the perfect climate...it is your space.

What sounds can you hear? Is there music or the hum of nature?

Are there any animals in your sacred space?

Is it light or dark? Is it daytime or night time? You are in control...

This is your own personal sacred space that you can visit during meditation at any time. You can also make changes at any point, and the space can grow with you.

Use the space to connect with your inner thoughts and feelings. Use the space to seek answers to questions or issues that need clarity. Use the space to just be...

When you are ready slowly come back to this reality, wriggling your fingers and toes and gently open your eyes, but know that the space you have created will always be there when you need it.

Seascape Meditation

Make yourself comfortable and relax.

Close your eyes and focus on your breathing, deep breaths in and deep breaths out.

As your room around you dissipates you find yourself standing on a stony beach. It is early in the morning and the beach is empty. It is warm, but the air feels fresh and alive and you can taste the salt on the light breeze.

The sound of the waves gently splashing on the shore is on the edge of your thoughts and you can hear faint cries of one or two seagulls as you notice them circling high above you.

There is a slight breeze that ruffles your hair.

You look around the area. To your left is a high cliff face, white with chalk and the glint of flint stone chips embedded in the rock.

To your right is a long stretch of open beach, colourful with pebbles, shingle and shells.

You make your way first down to the water's edge. Look at the ground and find something to drop into the surf as an offering. It might be a pretty pebble, a shell or a piece of driftwood. Pick up your offering and gently throw it into the waves as you ask for a blessing from the ocean, with her powers of release and cleansing.

When you are ready you turn and start to walk slowly along the shoreline with the vast expanse of pebbly beach stretching out in front of you.

The stones are interspersed with small green bushes and wild flowers. As you walk, take notice of what is around you on the seashore, in the stones, the plants and any animals or birds that might appear. If you have any questions for the ocean ask them too...

When you have walked far enough and received the answers that

75

you need, turn and thank the ocean, then slowly return to this reality...wriggling your fingers and toes and gently opening your eyes.

If You Go Down to the Woods Meditation

Make yourself comfortable and relax.

Close your eyes and focus on your breathing, deep breaths in and deep breaths out.

As your world around you dissipates you find yourself standing on a dirt track winding ahead of you into a dense forest. The scent on the air is heavy with the smell of leaves, soil and forest plants. The ground is wet and it feels and looks as if there has just been a heavy rainfall.

You start to follow the track into the trees...up above you the branches and leaves form a protective canopy. You listen...you can hear the sounds of the forest, the leaves whispering, the birds chattering and the special kind of soothing stillness that a large forest brings.

You follow the dirt track as it winds through the trees, feeling the leaf mulch under foot.

Keep your ears open for special sounds and your eyes open for gifts the forest might want to give you...

As you continue to walk the pathway opens up into a clearing. The sunlight beams down in shafts onto a large fallen tree, it lays on its side and provides somewhere for you to stop and sit.

Make yourself comfortable and sit for a while soaking up the magical energy of the forest...

As you sit, a large majestic stag enters the clearing and his eyes lock with yours...a connection...an understanding...

He stands looking directly at you for what feels like an eternity, but all of a sudden he turns and in the blink of an eye he is gone.

He had a reason for connecting with you, a message maybe or an answer that you were looking for.

When you are ready you get up and follow the direct pathway back out of the clearing and back through the forest the way that you came. Eventually you reach the edge of the forest, where you started from.

Slowly bring yourself back to this reality, wriggling your fingers and toes and gently open your eyes.

On a Mountain Top Meditation

Make yourself comfortable and relax.

Close your eyes and focus on your breathing, deep breaths in and deep breaths out.

As your world around you dissipates you find yourself at the foot of a cold, grey looking mountain. You are surrounded by fallen rocks thrown haphazardly onto the grassy earth. The sun is shining in a clear blue sky and the air smells beautifully fresh and clean with a hint of wild flowers.

As you look at the rocks you notice a gap that looks like a pathway, so you make your way over to it. As you pass between the rocks the scenery opens up to show you a narrow winding pathway that leads up the mountain side...so you follow it...

Either side of you are rocks and grassy mounds sprinkled with tiny beautiful wild flowers and visiting those flowers are busy bees filling the air with their heady buzzing sound. They are joined by multicoloured butterflies dancing between the flowers.

Occasionally as you walk a bird flies low across your line of vision and one or two of them land to perch on the rocks, watching you as you walk.

Listen to the sounds and look out for the gifts from Mother Nature as you follow the track upwards...

The track takes a sharp bend and as you turn the corner you find yourself at the very top of the mountain. It feels as if you are on the very top of the world.

A slight breeze comes across the top of the rock and it seems as if

it is blowing away all your worries and troubles. You hold your arms out and let the wind blow around you.

As you look around you can see the whole landscape...

When you are ready you turn and start to make your way back down the mountain, following the track that you came up on as it winds down slowly heading towards the base of the mountain to the point that you started from.

Slowly bring yourself back to this reality, wriggling your fingers and toes and gently open your eyes.

In the Desert Meditation

Make yourself comfortable and relax.

Close your eyes and focus on your breathing, deep breaths in and deep breaths out.

As your world around you dissipates you find yourself barefoot in the sand and it is warm, very warm. You can feel the sun on your face, your arms, your back and it is pleasant and comforting. It makes you feel warm, fuzzy and welcome.

As you look around all you can see is sand...lots and lots of sand stretching off as far as the eye can see. However, not too far ahead of you is an outcrop of rocks so you head towards it. You walk slowly as the sand feels lovely to step on to and you enjoy the feel of the sun on your face.

Once you reach the rocks you find a flat space to sit down on and notice that in the gaps between the rocks nature has prevailed and small spiky plants have made a home.

As you sit enjoying the warmth you notice a slight movement out of the corner of your eye...then it is gone. Then you catch it again...slowly a bright green lizard makes its way along the rock next to you then stops and just sits, occasionally flicking its tongue in and out...suddenly darting forward to zap a fly out of the air and bringing it into its mouth to munch.

Just as quickly as it arrived the lizard turns and darts back into its hiding place under the rocks.

When you are ready you get up and walk back across the sand to where you started from.

Slowly bring yourself back to this reality, wriggling your fingers and toes and gently open your eyes.

Seasons Meditation – Spring

Make yourself comfortable and relax.

Close your eyes and focus on your breathing, deep breaths in and deep breaths out.

As your world around you dissipates you find yourself standing in a field. The grass is damp with dew beneath your feet and scattered across the field are lots of little clumps of pale yellow cowslips. The air is fresh with a bit of a nip, but not too cold. The sky is a pale blue with streaks of white clouds and a watery sun is shining.

You hear the noise of water running and loud splashes so you walk towards the sound to find a wide river running alongside the field. The noise you heard was a mother duck ushering her ducklings from the river bank and down into the water. You watch them as they swim in a convoy up the river following the flow.

The river bank is green and covered with more of the pretty yellow cowslips. You find a comfortable spot to sit down to watch the river as it slowly follows its course, bubbling and tumbling along.

Further up the river bank, just within your range of sight, you watch a fisherman set up his equipment. He gets himself organized and casts his line into the water with a satisfying plop, the float bobbing along with the tide of the river.

The flow of the river is slightly hypnotic and it carries your thoughts along with it…

When you are ready you get up and make your way back from the river bank across the field to your starting point.

Slowly bring yourself back to this reality, wriggling your fingers and toes and gently open your eyes.

Seasons Meditation – Summer

Make yourself comfortable and relax.

Close your eyes and focus on your breathing, deep breaths in and deep breaths out.

As your world around you dissipates you find yourself in a field. The grass is long and comes up to your knees, it is also interspersed with pretty wild flowers. The sky is a clear bright blue and the sun is warm and pleasant.

The air is filled with the buzzing of bees and flittering of butterflies as they hop from flower to flower.

You hear a splashing noise and follow it to a river that runs alongside the field. The splashes are being made by two otters playing on the river bank and jumping in and out of the river. You find a comfortable spot and sit down to watch them play...

Further along the river you see a long barge moored to the side, it is painted in beautiful bright colours with intricate flower patterns in reds, blues, greens and yellows. All along the roof of the boat are painted pots filled with overflowing plants, flowers and herbs.

You hear a bark and watch as a puppy dog comes out of the interior of the barge and runs around the deck finally flopping down on the roof between the plant pots for a nap.

You watch the river once more as it gurgles and meanders along its course...

Then when you are ready you get up and make your way from the riverbank and back across the field to where you started.

Slowly bring yourself back to this reality, wriggling your fingers and toes and gently open your eyes.

Seasons Meditation – Autumn

Make yourself comfortable and relax.

Close your eyes and focus on your breathing, deep breaths in and deep breaths out.

As your world around you dissipates you find yourself standing in a field. The grass around your feet lies flat and yellowing as it was cut a short while ago and the seed pods have long been dispersed. The sky is blue, but there are a few white and grey clouds although the sun is still warm.

You hear the noise of running water and follow it to a river that runs alongside the field. You find a comfortable spot and sit down.

As you watch the river you see the trees on the other side. They are glorious colours, the entire spectrum of autumnal hues; oranges, reds and yellows. Each one is gifting its leaves to the river so that they float on the surface making a beautiful mosaic pattern on the water, which is ever-changing in shape and design as the current of the water flows.

The pattern of leaves is then separated and sent churning as two ducks fly down and land with a splash onto the river in a flurry of water, leaves and feathers, quacking noisily as they land. The ducks then gracefully swim downstream with a ribbon of leaves in their wake.

You watch the river for a while longer then when you are ready you get up and make your way back from the riverbank to the field where you started.

Slowly bring yourself back to this reality, wriggling your fingers and toes and gently open your eyes.

Seasons Meditation – Winter

Make yourself comfortable and relax.

Close your eyes and focus on your breathing, deep breaths in and deep breaths out.

As your world around you dissipates you find yourself standing in a field. The air is crisp with a chill, but you don't feel the cold. The sky is grey, but a weak sun is pushing itself through the clouds.

Your feet crunch as they stand on fresh snowfall and you look around to see a white blanket of snow.

You hear a faint noise of running water so you follow the sound to a river that is flowing beside the field.

You find a tree stump on the bank of the river and make yourself comfortable. The river is not frozen, but is flowing slowly. The banks either side are covered in snow and the trees on the other side of the river are bare, making dark silhouettes on the landscape.

You watch as the river carries lumps of snow broken away from the sides of the bank along with the flow and the occasional twig or branch that has fallen in further up stream as the water moves it along bobbing and bumping along with the flow.

As you sit and watch the river it starts to snow, gently at first, a scattering of individual snowflakes. You hold out your hand and watch as each flake hits your skin and stays for a brief second then melts away.

When you are ready you get up and walk back from the river bank to the field where your journey started.

Slowly bring yourself back to this reality, wriggling your fingers and toes and gently open your eyes.

Healing Temple Meditation

Make yourself comfortable and relax.

Close your eyes and focus on your breathing, deep breaths in and deep breaths out.

As your world around you dissipates you find yourself in what looks to be a temple. There are stone pillars all around you with beautiful carvings. The floor beneath your feet is a breathtaking mosaic made up from tiny pieces of brightly coloured tiles creating an amazing swirling pattern.

You then look up and realize that although you are surrounded by walls, the top of the temple is open to the sky, which is a deep midnight blue and littered with bright sparkling stars. It is then that you notice each of the stone pillars has a large flaming torch to light up the room you are in.

Then you hear a beautiful sound, the soft soothing strings of a harp...so you follow the notes through the temple to a large room that is the colour of a bright blue summer sky. In the centre of the room is a sunken bath filled with the clearest, brightest blue water and floating with pink and red rose petals. The scent of the bath water is captivating and on the side of the bath is a huge fluffy towel and you just know that it is meant for you.

Stepping into the bath the warm scented water draws you in further until you are lying comfortably submerged in its healing soothing waters. You can still hear the harp music and the combination of the beautiful sound, the scents and warm water starts to heal your mind, your body and your soul...

You can feel your worries, grief, pain and any emotional troubles just melting away...

You lay in complete bliss and allow the temple bath to work its healing magic...

You step out from the water and wrap yourself in the large welcoming towel that feels like a big soft hug.

When you are ready you leave the bath and walk back through the temple giving a word of thanks for the healing received.

Then slowly come back to this reality, wriggling your fingers and toes and gently open your eyes.

Earth Elemental Meditation

Make yourself comfortable and relax.

Close your eyes and focus on your breathing, deep breaths in and deep breaths out.

As your world around you dissipates you find yourself at the *entrance to a cave. It is night time and the dark blue sky is filled with stars and a full moon shines her light for you.*

You hear a noise from within the cave...you are not scared, but you are also intrigued...then you hear a voice say: 'Come.' It invites you inside. You enter the cave, which is dark at first, but the further in you go the brighter it is. The walls appear to be covered in crystals and some of them are glowing to provide light in the darkness.

Towards the back of the cave you notice a figure and as it becomes clearer you see a small man clothed in dark earthy colours; greens and browns. He has dark, wrinkled skin and a long beard...a gnome of the earth.

He gestures for you to follow him and turns heading deeper into the cave...so you follow... The ground is bare earth and the walls are cool to touch, embedded with crystals. The air is clear, but with a dry earthy scent.

You follow further into the cave until all of a sudden the cave tunnel opens up into a huge cavern...the sight takes your breath away...crystals of every size, colour and shape cover every bit of the walls and the ceiling...shining, sparkling and glistening.

The gnome beckons you over and indicates for you to sit on the floor in the centre. As you sit and gaze in wonder you hear soft chanting...the crystals are singing to you...listen carefully...

When you are ready the gnome appears again and you get up to follow him. He leads you back out of the cavern and down the tunnel to the cave and back to where you started. Just before he turns to leave he puts a small crystal in your hand...

Slowly come back to this reality, wriggling your fingers and toes and gently open your eyes.

Air Elemental Meditation

Make yourself comfortable and relax.

Close your eyes and focus on your breathing, deep breaths in and deep breaths out.

As your world around you dissipates you find yourself lying comfortably on soft green grass on the top of a hill with tall grasses swaying around you. The sky is a clear blue with wispy white clouds and there is a slight warm breeze.

You can feel the warm sun on your skin and the breeze that is moving the grasses around you… As you lay there start to focus on your breathing, listen to the sound that you make when you inhale and exhale… Feel the clean fresh air as it enters your body and travels down to your lungs…

Watch the delicate almost translucent clouds as the breeze carries them across the sky… What shapes can you see?

As you watch the clouds one or two of them appear to detach from the rest and start to float downwards…towards you…

One of the wisps of cloud brushes across your face and you feel an instant connection, a gentle whisper of energy…the word 'sylph' enters your mind…

The sylphs bring with them intellect and intuition…if you have any questions that you need insight on ask them now…or wait and see what information they have to pass on to you…

As the sylphs start to move away…floating back up towards the sky…you feel refreshed and energized…

When you are ready bring yourself back to this reality, wriggling your fingers and toes and gently open your eyes.

Fire Elemental Meditation

Make yourself comfortable and relax.

Close your eyes and focus on your breathing, deep breaths in and deep breaths out.

As your world around you dissipates you find yourself sitting in front of a large bonfire. It is night time and the sky is dark, the weather is cold, but you are wrapped up warm and you can feel the heat from the fire.

Listen…you can hear the sounds of the fire, the sparks, crackles and pops as the flames transform the wood into smouldering hot charcoal and then ashes...sending tiny sprinkles of fire and ash upwards in the wind.

You make yourself comfortable on the ground and sit and watch the flames...

The blaze fills your view and the flames create their dance in front of you, twisting and turning, the colours ranging from bright reds, to oranges, to yellows and whites...

A shape starts to form within the centre of the bonfire...several shapes in fact...small, developing not quite into human form, but almost...salamanders...the fiery elementals of the flame...

You can hear their voices calling out to you. The salamander brings passion, creativity and strength... What do they wish to share with you?

When you have finished communing with the salamanders they drift back into the flames of the fire leaving you feeling inspired and full of energy.

When you are ready come back to this reality, wriggling your fingers and toes and gently open your eyes.

Water Elemental Meditation

Make yourself comfortable and relax.

Close your eyes and focus on your breathing, deep breaths in and deep breaths out.

As your world around you dissipates you find yourself on the edge of a rock pool beside the shoreline of a large azure blue ocean. The sky is a beautiful blue and the sun is shining.

The rock pool is edged with flat grey stones large enough for you to sit comfortably on, with white-yellow sand all around scattered with pretty sea shells.

You sit and gaze into the depths of the rock pool, the water is a dark blue and appears to be extremely deep...you watch as the surface ripples slightly...

Dark green seaweed lines the inner rocks around the edge of the rock pool and one or two small crabs wander in and out seeking food and shelter from the sun.

The surface of the water starts to move even more...until you are surprised to see a large tail flip up out of the water and cause a gentle splash... A few seconds later a haunting face appears from beneath the water...gorgeous long dark hair and captivating eyes...you are face to face with an undine...an elemental of the sea...

You are speechless for a few moments until the undine breaks the silence... It does not appear to speak out loud, instead the words seem to appear in your mind... Undines bring all the magic and spirit of the ocean, emotions and expression...thoughts, images and words fill your head...

Then as suddenly as the undine appeared it is gone...leaving just a few ripples once again on the surface of the pool.

You feel enlightened...

When you are ready slowly come back to this reality, wriggling your fingers and toes and gently open your eyes.

Grounding Meditation

You can use this as a dedicated meditation or it can be used in a shorter form at any time during your day when you feel the need to stop for a few seconds and ground and centre, to release any negative energy, anger or grief and to find your inner peace again. Make yourself comfortable and relax.

Close your eyes and focus on your breathing, deep breaths in and deep breaths out.

As your room around you dissipates you find yourself in a glade in the middle of a lush green forest. Listen to the sounds of the forest around you and breathe in the earthy scent of the forest floor.

As you stand silently, bare feet connected with the forest floor, you feel the urge to wriggle your toes in the soil... As you do so your feet begin to send down roots, gently and slowly creeping through the earth downwards, feel the sensation of connecting with the ground…

You feel the need to stretch your arms out wide, a really big long stretch…and as you do so your fingers begin to sprout leaves, your arms becoming sturdy branches and your face turning towards the sky…

You roots continue to search, to seek out the water and minerals beneath the soil, growing ever downwards towards the very centre of the world, to its core.

When your roots reach the middle of the world feel the energy and power, know that the earth is happy for you to connect with that energy and draw some back up through your roots for yourself. Feel the force and vigour being drawn back up through your roots into your feet and surging around each and every part of your body, revitalizing, energizing and connecting you with the stability and strength of the earth.

When you have had your fill of earth energy slowly and gently begin to draw your roots back upwards, back through the soil, back through the earth and carefully into your feet.

Slowly draw the leaves back into your fingers and the branches back into your arms…

When you are ready thank Mother Earth for her gifts and gently come back to this reality.

If you feel you have too much energy on board just place your hands on the floor palms facing downwards and release the excess back into the ground.

A Meditation to Meet an Animal Guide or Messenger
Make yourself comfortable and relax.

Close your eyes and focus on your breathing, deep breaths in and deep breaths out.

As your room around you dissipates you find yourself in a large cave. There are natural handmade rugs on the floor and rough paintings on the cave walls.

There is a fire in the centre with a pot hanging over it, and various herbs and flowers hanging from the roof to dry. You can smell musky and aromatic scents.

Behind you, you can hear water. As you turn you see that the whole side of the cave is open to the sky. It is night time and dark, but the whole sky is scattered with beautiful stars.

You make your way to the edge and realize you are on a ledge, high above the sea. Waves are crashing onto the rocks below, and rainbows are thrown up along with the waves.

You notice a path curving downwards through the rock; you start to follow this path downwards, the waves crashing onto the rocks beside you. You can feel the vibrations and power of the water and can smell and taste the salt, feeling the fine mist on your skin.

As you reach the bottom of the path you step out onto the shore. It is more peaceful here, calm and relaxing.

As you adjust to your surroundings you notice that behind you now is a forest of beautiful old trees, with a blanket of wild herbs beneath their feet. Hear leaves rustling in the trees. Smell the scent of the wild herbs that the air brings to you. In amongst the herbs are strands of washed-up seaweed, shells, pebbles and twigs.

You wander along the boundary, looking at the ocean on one side, the trees on the other. Take note of the leaves, the branches, the shells, and the herbs – all that you see around you.

You notice a large, flat rock just on the boundary between the sea and the forest. You make your way to it and sit down. Behind you are the sounds of the forest; in front of you is the ocean. The waves have a rhythmic, soothing sound, like the slow beating of a drum.

Let your thoughts drift just for a moment and take in the sounds of the sea, the sounds of the forest and the scent of sea air, and wild herbs. Take it all in.

Movement appears in the corner of your vision, you turn and look – it may have come from the sea, it may have come from the beach, it may have come from the forest or even from the sky...

It is a creature...

As it comes closer you can make out what creature it is, its colour and its markings. This is an animal spirit guide. One that is meant for you. It has a message for you. You listen...

When you have listened to its message the creature indicates that you are to follow it back up the pathway to the cave. You stand and then follow it back along the beach to the base of the cliff. It leads you up the narrow pathway to the ledge of the cave.

There is a choice now, this animal guide may come with you, or it may turn and depart.

If it stays it is a totem guide and will be with you for as long as you need it. Even if you forget it is there; or withdraw from it, it will still walk in the shadows guiding and guarding you. If the animal turns and departs then it was a spirit messenger, take note of the message it gave you.

The cave dissipates and your room reappears around you. Stretch your arms and come back into focus.

Dragon Meditation

Make yourself comfortable and relax.

Close your eyes and focus on your breathing, deep breaths in and deep breaths out.

Your world around you dissipates and you find yourself in a clearing. In the distance you can see mountains and what looks like a volcano top with smoke creeping out of its crater. Behind you is a large dense forest and to one side you turn to see a large lake.

Look up towards the sky and see the storm clouds rolling in from over the mountain tops, although the sun is still trying to break through and long shafts of light beam down on the surface of the lake making it glint and sparkle.

You realise you are not alone. Flying high above you are shapes that look like large birds, on a second look you realise they are dragons, dark shapes weaving in and out of the clouds.

Then you hear crashing sounds coming from the forest and realise that behind the trees large dragons are moving around. But you don't feel afraid.

Splashing from the lake draws your attention and you notice that some of the glints in the water are actually dragons swimming and splashing, breaking the surface of the water.

A loud roaring sound draws your attention to the mountain tops and you see that diving in and out of the volcano crater are dragons, breathing long streams of flame as they dive.

Then on the shoreline of the lake you realise what you thought were sandy rocks you see now are large desert dragons sunning themselves.

Stand for a moment and draw on the powers of all these different dragons. Reach out with your mind and see if one of them makes a connection with you.

If one does, ask it to join you where you are standing. Wait until it stands beside you then ask for permission to ask it some questions. If it agrees then ask what you want to know.

Once you are finished, thank the dragon for its presence, guidance and wisdom and bid it farewell. It may tell you that it is your dragon guardian now and you can call upon it any time, it may not.

Know that you can always come back to the land of dragons for guidance.

Slowly bring your focus back to the present, shake your arms and legs and open your eyes.

Quick-Fire Meditation Themes

Here I am sharing some ideas for you to meditate upon. They aren't full guided meditations just hints or suggestions giving you a subject to base your own meditation on...make yourself comfortable, take a few deep breaths in and out and then run the subject suggestion around in your head and see where your subconscious mind takes you...

- A pathway...brick, stone, pebble or a dirt track...leading to?
- A dark night sky sprinkled with stars and a full moon.
- A bright blue sky and a flock of birds heading off into the distance.
- A pool of dark water...gaze into it...what do you see?
- A large sprawling oak tree with winding roots.
- A crossroads...which way will you turn?
- A small boat tied up on the riverbank...you climb in...
- You are in the basket of a hot air balloon...
- Sitting in front of a large bonfire, watch the flames...
- Standing at the edge of a forest...do you go in?
- You are riding a horse in amongst a group of wild horses...galloping...
- You are very tiny and riding on the back of a dragonfly...
- You are standing on top of a tall mountain looking down at the scenery around you.
- You can hear beautiful music...
- You are looking into a mirror...what do you see?
- You are under the water swimming with shoals of fish.
- Standing in a hallway full of doors...which one will you choose to open?
- You meet an old wise woman (or man)...what questions will you ask them?

- Walk around a spiral maze...what thoughts come to you as you walk and what is at the centre?
- You are a bird...soaring high above the ground...
- Standing in front of a blank canvas with a palette of paints and brushes...
- Lying on your back on the ground looking up at the clouds...what do you see?
- You are sitting in a chair facing an empty chair. Someone comes and sits in the empty chair...who is it and what do you want to say to them?
- You push open a gate that sits in an old brick wall...what do you find on the other side?
- In front of you is an old fashioned circus tent, you lift the flap and walk through...
- The music is playing, people around you are laughing and having fun and you are dancing...dancing without care or thought...
- You see a large old leather bound book on a wooden desk...you can hear a scratching noise as if the story is still being written inside...you open the book...
- A playground lies before you with swings, slides, round-abouts and a sandpit...there is no one around except you...
- Pick an image from nature...a tree, a flower, a river, mountains, a still pond, a leaf...focus on it...
- Sitting on the beach watching the sun rise...or the sun set...

Closing...

At the end of the day we all have busy lives, but if you can just squeeze in a five minute meditation each day you will really feel the benefit. Although I have given many suggestions in this book on how to meditate, how to sit and everything else bar what colour wallpaper you need, this journey is yours so make it personal. Go with what works for you, there is no right or wrong way...just your way...

Some forms of meditation can be hard work, some take years of practise and others may not suit you at all, please don't be disheartened. You may find it helpful to contact a local group a quick internet search should hopefully find support in your area or online guidance.

Useful books

Healing Crystals by Cassandra Eason

A Kitchen Witch's World of Magical Plants & Herbs by Rachel Patterson

Crystal Prescriptions by Judy Hall

Hedge Riding by Harmonia Saille

Animal Speak by Ted Andrews

Magical Beast by Marie Bruce

Power Animal Meditations by Scully

Shaman Pathways – The Celtic Chakras by Elen Sentier

The Chakras Made Easy by Hilary H Carter

Druidry and Meditation by Nimue Brown

The Complete Idiot's Guide to the Akashic Records by Dr Synthia Andrews & Colin Andrews

Bibliography

Pagan Portals: Kitchen Witchcraft
Grimoire of a Kitchen Witch
Pagan Portals: Hoodoo Folk Magic
Pagan Portals: Moon Magic
A Kitchen Witch's World of Magical Plants & Herbs
A Kitchen Witch's World of Magical Foods

Moon Books invites you to begin or deepen your encounter with Paganism, in all its rich, creative, flourishing forms.